Can I Ask You A QUESTION?

Sharing Christ Effectively

PRESTON CONDRA | KELLY CONDRA

Can I Ask You a Question? – Louisiana:
Sharing Christ Effectively
Louisiana Baptists

Louisiana Baptists Leadership Team:
Dr. Steve Horn, Executive Director
Keith Manuel, Evangelism & Church Growth Team Leader

Production and Design: Sufficient Word Ministries and
Madison Lux *upwork.com/fl/madisonlux*

**To order, send shipping address, contact information, and number
of copies requested to publisher@sufficientwordpublishing.com**

Louisiana Edition: September 2022
ISBN: 978-1-946245-15-1

TABLE OF CONTENTS

*   Familiarity with the Index of Objections is what makes this book
useful as a resource handbook.

FOREWORD

"Asking the QUESTION" is what every professing Christian is called to do. Yet, too often, a lack of confidence results in missed opportunities and absence of pursuit.

Louisiana Baptists are excited to partner with Preston and Kelly Condra in an evangelism book series called *Can I Ask You a Question?* Strategically focusing on three characteristics critical to sharing God's Word, the Condras have succinctly presented simple steps which equip Christians to take action and share the Gospel with *confidence, clarity,* and *caring.*

Personal evangelism is closely tied to apologetics, especially today. So, genuinely caring and speaking truth with clarity and confidence is crucial to Gospel-sharing. That is exactly what this series provides for churches, individuals, and small groups. The materials include this book—*Can I Ask You a Question?*—an apologetics handbook to answer objections to the Gospel, *Asking the Question,* an action guide for evangelism training, and *Answers,* a resource to give away when witnessing. All the materials are based on the Word of God and include training on how to initiate conversations, respond to objections, find scriptural answers, and share the Gospel of Christ in a no-pressure and straight-forward manner. Eternal life is at stake! Although we know every witnessing event will not result in salvation, none will be saved unless we step out and tell others about Jesus, and... we are commanded to do it.

Given the magnitude of our gift of salvation and relationship with Jesus Christ, there is nothing that should be more natural to us than to share the Good News. Using 1 Corinthians 15:1-4, this material shows exactly how to approach evangelism naturally and simply. Through their relationship with Jesus Christ, Christians can be capable evangelists.

I believe the *Can I Ask You a Question?* series follows God's Word, underscores His plan, addresses our fears, and offers Christians renewed confidence and timely relevance for effective evangelism. It is an excellent tool to assist churches to foster individual growth and small group education on the power, privilege, and responsibility of personal evangelism.

Every Christian needs a wake-up call to personal evangelism, and it starts by "Asking the Question" with *confidence, clarity,* and *caring.*

Keith Manuel, Ph.D.
Louisiana Baptists
Director
Evangelism & Church Growth Team
LouisianaBaptists.org
KeithManuel.com

INTRODUCTION

FOR THE WORK OF THE MINISTRY

*For the perfecting of the saints, for the
work of the ministry, for the edifying of
the body of Christ.* (Eph 4:12)

In just a few years, the world has completely changed. Americans have witnessed a massive societal evolution, and many find themselves in stunned silence on a regular basis, wondering, "How can the things we are seeing be so?" As the nation has changed, so have its churches. The foundation of a seemingly sudden cultural shift was actually laid decades ago, when support for the authority and sufficiency of God's word waned in the pulpits of our nation. The church has been marginalized and Anti-Christ philosophies have become more prominent than Christian values. Furthermore, talking to others about these changes becomes ever more difficult. Satan, the Ruler of this Age and the promoter of "political correctness" and "tolerance" discourages discussion of either our earthly freedoms or our heavenly position, both of which hamper his agenda.

As the culture embraces ever more shocking behaviors and beliefs, similar moral flexibility increases within the church.

Some church attendees reverse their opinion on a moral issue as soon as someone they love begins to practice a particular sin. The spread of post-modern thinking with its moral relativism makes it increasingly difficult to communicate the absolute truths of scripture. With this cultural shift, assumptions regarding evangelism must also change. For example, we, the authors, rarely ask anyone if he is a "Christian," because it does not mean what it used to. We cannot assume that fellow church members share our worldview or even believe that the Bible is true. Some who attend church on Sunday fight for ungodly causes on Monday.

Believers fear for their friendships, their livelihoods, and even their freedom for standing on biblical principles. Not wanting to cause offense, attract the label of "religious fanatic," or be the next victim of world-wide media attention, many avoid religious discussion altogether. Others are willing, but tell us they are not equipped to handle the questions and objections which may arise in a conversation about their faith. As Christian beliefs and practices have been systematically eliminated from our society, we feel strongly that more must be done to prepare believers for evangelism and to integrate witnessing more fully into everyday life.

If the nation's altered worldview, society's hostility, and the risk of personal attack are not barriers enough, those who oppose the Gospel are not the only obstacle to successful evangelism. Some segments of Christendom promote "simplified" versions of the Gospel, altered with well-intentions, but lacking in clarity and accuracy. So, the believer's dilemma is that while the culture increasingly opposes Christianity, our call to proclaim the Gospel remains, and the world's need for it grows. Although we will face resistance to the Gospel of Christ, it is possible to discuss it without being found offensive. There are many people who have questions and who want to talk about faith, the Bible, and eternity. They may not dare to start a "politically incorrect" conversation themselves, but they will be glad that someone else is willing. Our goal as authors is to help Christians get conversations started and to provide an effective way to share the Gospel.

Reported Barriers to Witnessing

When witnessing is discussed, Christians consistently state the same concerns:

- I don't know how to start a conversation, especially without causing offense.
- I am not sure what to say.
- I am not equipped to handle objections.

Because we care about the eternal destiny of those around us, we, as Christians, can open a conversation and determine a person's interest in spiritual things by simply asking him a question. What to say and how to ask those opening questions are detailed in the companion guide. The focus of this book is two-fold: It emphasizes a clear, thoroughly explained Gospel, and it functions as a handbook for answering objections to the Gospel. A list of objections can be found in the appendix of this book.

Effective Evangelism

A Christian witness must thoroughly understand the elements of the Gospel in order to accurately share it with others and answer questions about it. First and foremost, we must share the Gospel with **clarity**. Chapter One of this book explains the elements of the Gospel message and several aspects of salvation itself, such as the new birth and the source of sin. Nothing saves apart from the Gospel of Christ, the power of God unto salvation; therefore, this book promotes the use of that passage which Paul calls "the gospel by which also ye are saved," 1 Corinthians 15:1-4. There is no benefit in sharing an inaccurate message; doing so can sow confusion and even result in false conversions.

Bearing witness to the saving power of the Gospel can be an intimidating proposition. The second help that this book provides is the **confidence** to initiate conversations. This evangelism handbook is a nearly exhaustive resource to answering objections to the Gospel, using concise explanations and several supporting Bible verses. With its quick-reference Index of Objections, a Christian witness can confidently turn to the topic of an objection and ask a hearer if he would like to see what the Bible says about it. This directs attention to the testimony of scripture and away from any disagreement between the witness and the hearer.

Thirdly, the companion guide offers several ways to approach people without forcing unnatural conversations, creating awkward situations, or causing offence. It teaches Christians how to personalize the question they will ask so that evangelistic opportunities are suited to the real-life circumstances of the witness and the hearer. Its **caring** approach facilitates the best outcome in witnessing situations.

The Gospel of Christ has Five Elements

This book divides the Gospel of Christ into five easy-to-remember elements:

- Who Jesus is
- What He did for us

- Why we need it
- How we get it
- Where we find it

These elements overlap: verses in one section may help with other objections, so familiarizing yourself with the objections will increase the effectiveness of this handbook. Lines at the end of each section provide a place for notes.

By Faith Alone

Nothing is required for salvation other than faith in the death, burial, and resurrection of Jesus Christ for the purpose of salvation from sin. The Gospel can be simply believed with the faith of a child. It can also be misunderstood in many ways—as evidenced by the many objections to it. The philosophy of this book is that Christians are to trust the testimony of God's word in evangelism just as we are to do in every other area of life. God graciously allows the members of the body of Christ to be His partners in ministry, but people cannot be argued into heaven; they are to be offered the truth with love. It is not the purpose of this book to facilitate arguments or debates, but only to provide an effective way to explain the Gospel and answer objections. Each saint does his part by initiating conversations about biblical topics, thoroughly explaining the Gospel, offering scriptural answers, and praying for every hearer. We know it is the Holy Spirit who draws mankind through the preaching of the Gospel as He convicts each sinner of his need. With clarity, confidence, and caring, Christians can fulfill the calling to function as ministers of the Gospel of Christ and facilitate the Spirit's work in each heart.

Satan wants us to believe that we are not equipped to share the Gospel, or that it is too risky to do so, but it need not be so. We are to be a light to a dying world! As members of the body of Christ, we are to build up one another in the work of the ministry. May this book be helpful to the saints in effectively sharing the good news with a world that desperately needs it.

> *Moreover, brethren, I declare unto you the gospel which I preached unto you, which also ye have received, and wherein ye stand; By which also ye are saved ...* (1 Cor 15:1-2)

O N E

THE GOSPEL BY WHICH WE ARE SAVED

The Gospel of Christ

*M*oreover, brethren, I declare unto you the gospel which I preached unto you, which also ye have received, and wherein ye stand; 2 **By which also ye are saved,** if ye keep in memory what I preached unto you, unless ye have believed in vain. 3 For I delivered unto you first of all that which I also received, how that Christ died for our sins according to the scriptures; 4 And that he was buried, and that he rose again the third day according to the scriptures: 5 And that he was seen of Cephas, then of the twelve: 6 After that, he was seen of above five hundred brethren at once; of whom the greater part remain unto this present, but some are fallen asleep. 7 After that, he was seen of James; then of all the apostles. 8 And last of all he was seen of me also, as of one born out of due time. (1 Cor 15:1-8)*

The Main Event

When asking someone a question about his faith, the goal is to get to the "good news." As Christians, we initiate conversations in order to learn more about the beliefs of those with whom we work, play, live near, and meet in daily life. It is vital that the content of this "good news," or Gospel message, is accurately conveyed because it is that "by which" we are saved. Stated fully within 1 Corinthians 15:1-8, this saving message was given a title by Paul in Romans 1:16; he called it the "Gospel of Christ," and described it as "the power of God unto salvation." Although other

> ... the gospel of Christ ... it is the power of God unto salvation ... (from Ro 1:16)

verses such as John 3:16 and Ephesians 2:8-9 contain additional information about salvation, 1 Corinthians 15: 3-4 is the essential core of the Gospel, namely the death, burial, and resurrection of Jesus Christ for our sins. It is the object of faith for salvation, and it is the message that we are to share.

For the purposes of this book, we refer to the Gospel as 1 Corinthians 15:1-4, because we believe that verses 1-2 are worthy of inclusion in a Gospel presentation. They identify the passage as the saving Gospel message, and provide a warning about believing in vain—a factual belief without the intended purpose of salvation. We sometimes include verses 5-8 which declare proof of the resurrection verified by hundreds of witnesses.

Because Satan can twist every aspect of the Gospel, knowing and understanding its elements is essential for recognizing and answering misdirected belief, misunderstandings, and various erroneous ideas about salvation. Many unsaved people are assumed to be Christian until a conversation arises in which they express beliefs that contradict the Gospel. We have met sincere people who initially seem to agree that Jesus died for their sins, but upon further discussion, they reveal definitions of Jesus, salvation, or other Gospel elements which differ from the biblical meaning of these terms. Because each part of the Gospel is necessary, misunderstanding or denying part of the Gospel is equivalent to not believing the Gospel at all. Therefore, we exhort believers to use 1 Corinthians 15:1-4 when witnessing; we can do so with confidence if we know it well.

Although the Gospel contains necessary elements, it is not simply a formula. Each hearer of the Gospel has his own ideas about God, eternity, and religion, as well as many questions. Regardless of the objections raised or questions asked in a witnessing situation, a Christian who thoroughly knows the Gospel can direct the conversation back to the Gospel element to which the question relates. Doing so keeps the conversation Bible-centered, making God the authority, not the Christian witness. We wish not only to help Christians offer a clear and accurate Gospel, but to avoid making the conversation a battle of wills or a debate.

The five elements of the Gospel of Christ are labeled in this book as who, what, why, how, and where. Briefly, they are as follows:

- **Who:** Jesus Christ, God the Son, the one and only Savior of sinners, and the one and only way of salvation.
- **What:** The death on the cross, burial, and resurrection of Jesus Christ as a substitute for the sins of mankind, taking upon Himself the wrath of God against sin.
- **Why:** Jesus died for us because every human being is a sinner and under penalty of death for sinning against God. As finite human beings we cannot "make up for" or "undo" our sins and are, therefore, facing eternal suffering in the lake of fire, the permanent residence of those who will pay for their own sins.

- **How:** We can be saved from the penalty of sin by grace through faith. God graciously grants deliverance to each who believes the Gospel of Christ, 1 Corinthians 15:1-4, and who does so for the purpose of his own salvation, apart from works of any kind.
- **Where:** Twice in the Gospel we find the phrase, "according to the scriptures," a reference to the source of the saving message. Because the Bible is the revelation of Jesus Christ and the source of the Gospel, disbelief in the Bible can be a barrier to accepting the truth of its message.

By focusing on the Gospel message, we are attempting to show those with whom we speak that our goal is not to win an argument about religion; what we care about is their eternal destiny.

The Backstory

In addition to the essential elements of the Gospel of Christ, there are several biblical teachings which underpin the Gospel. These are helpful for believers to understand in order to explain some objections to it. These teachings include the meaning of spiritual birth, the substitutionary sacrifice of Jesus, man's position in the family of Adam, the placement of the believer into the body of Christ, the necessity of the faith system for salvation, and the Bible as God's written revelation of Himself.

There is great benefit in understanding the Gospel thoroughly, but no benefit in assuming that those with whom we share the Gospel already possess accurate definitions of its elements. Of all the potential objections to the Gospel, the most common is the mainstay of false religion: works for salvation. A broader understanding of the doctrines related to salvation can be used to show that salvation by faith is a spiritual transaction, and is, therefore, distinct from human efforts of any kind.

Because the Bible is the exclusive source of every Christian doctrine, we find that witnessing goes more smoothly if we begin by asking a hearer about his view of scripture. The balance of this chapter, starting with the case for addressing the Bible as a potential objection, contains explanations of some of the supporting doctrines of the Gospel, as well as the Gospel elements themselves.

The Authoritative Source of the Gospel is the Bible

Creation itself reveals the existence of a Creator, but the general revelation of God's existence does not reveal His identity, nor how to enter into a relationship with Him. We need more information than the creation around us to know who God is. So, how can we know Him, and know that His message is true? He provided two proofs of Himself: He walked among us in the person of Jesus

> Ask a hearer about his view of scripture.

Christ, and He provided a written record revealing Himself. The Bible is our trustworthy historical record which reveals God the Son and the message of salvation, the Gospel of Christ.

The Gospel of Christ, found in 1 Corinthians 15:1-4, contains the phrase "according to the scriptures" twice, suggesting that the trustworthiness of the source of the message is inextricable from the facts of the saving message. For this reason, we encourage Christian witnesses to ask a hearer's opinion of the Bible when sharing the Gospel. Those who have a general respect for the Bible may be willing to consider what it says, while a person who does not trust the Bible may not be ready to believe its saving message or even listen to its testimony. From his perspective, he is being asked to entrust his eternal destiny to a message from an unreliable source.

Unbelief that is rooted in distrust of the Bible creates a dilemma for witnessing and an obstacle for salvation, since it is the Bible itself wherein all proof lies. An article or a book written to offer evidence of the Bible as a supernatural revelation from God and a reliable historical record may be a better place to begin with those who object to the Bible. Learning early if there is hostility or indifference toward the Bible can avoid frustration for both the Christian and the hearer in a witnessing situation. Discussing the trustworthiness of the Bible can help an initially dismissive objector realize that he has no concrete reasons for doubting its testimony. If, on the other hand, he voices strong objections, quoting verses of scripture may not be the best starting point for a discussion of faith and eternity. We would not tell a Christian witness not to quote scripture, as the Holy Spirit uses the words of scripture to teach us the truth of the Gospel (Jn 16:13). We ask only that Christians exercise discernment; a hearer might refuse to consider the word of God but be willing to learn why so many others believe it.

Christian Salvation is a Spiritual Birth

The biblical concept of a spiritual birth is one that we have found is not well understood, even among Christians. It is a unique teaching, one that was difficult for even a learned religious leader of Israel to understand (Jn 3:4). Although it may not be necessary to explain the details of spiritual birth when witnessing, a discussion about the Gospel often reveals what may be the world's most common religious belief, that one must perform rituals or good works to appease or impress "god." An explanation of the Christian spiritual birth is sometimes needed in order to distinguish religious works from spiritual salvation.

Christianity stands alone in teaching that no one has ever been saved by law-keeping, a clean life, or works of any kind. The Bible tells us instead that we must be "born again" (Jn 3:7). But Christians and non-Christians alike may hold views of Christianity which make it seem like a social activity or membership in a civic group. It is important for hearers to know that our faith is not simply a lifestyle of

> Outward traits cannot define Christianity; they are a result of it.

goodness, giving, and church attendance. While morality, helpfulness, and fellowship are meant to be products of a spiritual birth, there are many decent, philanthropic, community-minded non-Christians. Therefore, such outward traits cannot define Christianity; they are a result of it. It is possible for someone to give verbal assent to the death, burial, and resurrection of Jesus, while still holding on to a belief in works for salvation.

Helpful for comprehending the Christian spiritual birth is knowing more about birth and death according to scripture. For example, the death of a person does not result in his annihilation or non-existence. When a person's physical body stops functioning, that person lives on. Death can be viewed, therefore, as a separation. The material part of man, the body, is in the grave, separated from the immaterial soul and spirit, which continue to live.

The human spirit is the part of man which can be connected to God. God is the only source of spiritual life, which is why we refer to our relationship with Him as spiritual. A person can be physically alive and yet be spiritually dead because he is separated from the source of spiritual life (Eph 2:1). To be spiritually born means that one's human spirit is in communion with, meaning connected with, God. Other references to aspects of the born-again spiritual condition include "the new birth," being "born from above," "begotten again," "indwelt," and "regenerated." Awareness of the various terms can aid communication when witnessing.

Paradise Lost

In addition to knowing that being "born again" refers to our spiritual connection with God, we recommend that Christians know a little of humanity's background in relation to spirituality.

A brief history of human spiritual life begins with Adam, who was created sinless and in spiritual communion with God. God told Adam that if he ate from the tree of the knowledge of good and evil, he would die (Gen 3:3). But

> Adam ... begat a son ... after his image ... (from Gen 5:3)

Adam did not drop dead upon eating it. Although he *began* dying physically, his immediate death was spiritual. God could no longer commune with Adam's spirit because it was now tainted with sin.

When Adam ate from the tree, he had made a decision to act independently of God's will. His act of disobedience was sin, and, therefore, he became separated from a holy God who cannot commune with sin. Neither could God commune spiritually with any of Adam's descendants. Although Adam was created in the likeness of God, the Bible tells us that after he sinned, Adam's children were created in *his* likeness; they were fallen sinners (Gen 5:1-3). Having sinned, Adam no longer possessed the quality of being spiritually alive and, therefore, could not pass on to his descendants that which he no longer had. As a result of being part of Adam's family, all men are born separated from God, just as Adam became separated when he rebelled in the garden (Gen 3:6). This is why every person is born a sinner, and why the Bible refers to unsaved humanity as being "in Adam," a doctrine covered later in this chapter.

The intimate spiritual connection enjoyed by Adam could not be restored until sin no longer stood between God and man. The restoration of spiritual communion was accomplished when God the Son died for sin on the cross (Ro 5:10; 2 Cor 5:18-19). With all sin having been paid, God can now commune with any man who has accepted that payment for his own sins (1 Cor 15:22).

> Christianity is a spiritual birth.

In summary, all men are born spiritually dead, separated from God by sin, and in need of a savior. To escape the punishment for sin, we must each be cleansed from sin by accepting Jesus' payment for sin on our behalf. Upon believing the Gospel, we are no longer separated from God by sin. We are saved from damnation, made part of a spiritual family, able to enjoy a relationship with God, and destined for heaven.

Learning about the need for spiritual birth can be vital to a correct understanding of the Gospel. Those who see the Christian faith as simply a lifestyle choice may have convinced themselves and others that they are Christians, without having been born again. If they claim to be Christian, who would think to share the Gospel with them? But if they have not believed the Gospel, they remain separated from God. We believe that to fulfill the Christian calling to share the Gospel, we must do more than briefly mention the death, burial, and resurrection for sins. By asking hearers to tell us what they believe about the elements of the Gospel message, we can address any misunderstandings they have about it which are not readily apparent.

Jesus Christ is God the Son, the One and Only Savior of Mankind

Understanding the spiritual nature of the Christian faith is often needed to distinguish it from works when sharing the Gospel. But central to the Gospel message is the Savior Himself. Explaining Jesus is not easy. The Gospel verses do not plainly say "Jesus is God." But could someone be saved who denied that Jesus was God? If Jesus is simply a man and not God, could a person's faith in an ordinary man save him, even if that man was an extraordinary example of altruism, forgiveness, and love?

Because some hearers believe that Jesus was only a man, a Christian witness needs to be able to explain a few things about the Savior of mankind. Doing so is foundational to providing further explanation about what He did for us. For example, an ordinary man cannot also be mankind's savior. He would have no way to pay for the sins of others, because he would have his own to pay for. His death on a cross would not solve the problem of sin between God and man, because it would be followed by the penalty God requires for every man: eternal separation in the lake of fire (Rev 20:15). There must be something unique about the One who took the infinite sins of the world upon Himself. He was not just some great guy who died to set an example of sacrificial love or to make a statement about forgiveness, as some believe.

One way to address the need for the Savior to be God is to relay the enormity of the sin problem, as well as the seriousness of having offended God. Because the sins of mankind are a problem of infinite proportions, paying for those sins requires an infinite payment. Either a sinner will spend an infinity paying for sin (Rev 20:10-14), or his sins must be laid upon an infinite person. In other words, the Savior of the world would have to be our infinite God. Additionally, in order to be a substitute for mankind, and specifically a replacement for Adam as the head of the human family, the Savior would have to be a man. Jesus is the only one who fulfills both requirements: He is fully God, who took on a human nature and body to become fully man also (Phil 2:6, Col 2:9, Heb 2:6). In so doing, He was a just and infinite substitute for man and a sacrifice for the sins of mankind, making Himself the recipient of God's wrath against sin.

Jesus is God in the flesh, and contrary to the prevalent belief that Jesus is one of many equally valid ways of salvation, He is the one and only Savior of mankind. The Gospel is not compatible with, "You have your way; I have mine." Because of Jesus' exclusive claims, one cannot believe that there are other "saviors" or other ways to be saved while at the same time believing the Gospel (Acts 4:12, Jn 8:12, 10:9, 14:6).

> One cannot believe that there are other "saviors" or other ways to be saved while at the same time believing the Gospel.

A person who considers Jesus to be one religious prophet, messenger, or savior among many does not believe in the true Jesus Christ, but a false Christ of his own creation. Therefore, the object of that man's faith is vain, meaning it is of no use for the purpose of saving. The object of saving faith must be the correct object, namely, Jesus Christ, God the Son, the Savior of the world

(1 Cor 15:2, 2 Cor 11:4). When sharing the Gospel, asking a hearer to explain what he understands about Jesus is of great importance; he must understand in what and in whom he is being asked to place his faith for salvation.

Jesus Paid for Our Sins by Dying on a Cross

Jesus is at the center of the Gospel message. To be saved, one must believe in what He did: that He died for sins on a cross, was buried, and rose again, according to the scriptures. Some hearers will question what Jesus did and why He did it. For example, many people died on crosses; what was different about this death? Why was a cross the method of Jesus' death and what did it achieve?

Jesus had to die because the shedding of blood is the method that Almighty God chose for paying a debt to Him. Leviticus 17:11 informs us that life is in the blood, and we know that losing one's blood is certain death. Hebrews 9:22 teaches that without the shedding of blood is no remission, referring to the remission of sins. We see blood sacrifice after the fall in Genesis 4:3-5 and in the Law of Moses. When God the Son came to earth to be a sacrifice for all mankind, He took on a human body and shed His blood, giving His life for ours.

Jesus' death was unique because it fulfilled prophecy, allowing Jesus to be identified by Israel as its Messiah. The Bible does not explain why God chose crucifixion as the manner of death, but this horrific method does seem to highlight the seriousness of sin. Under the Law of Moses, dying on a tree signified being cursed by God, pointing to the destiny of all sinners (Deut 21:22-23, Gal 3:13, Jn 3:18).

Looking again to the first man, Adam, we can see what Jesus' death actually achieved. In 1 Corinthians 15:45, Jesus is called the "last Adam." 1 Corinthians 15:22 states, "For as in Adam all die, even so in Christ shall all be made alive." Jesus became Adam's substitute as head of the human race; when God the Father poured out His wrath against sin onto Jesus Christ, making Him sin for us, He was moving the accountability for sin to Jesus (2 Cor 5:21). Because Jesus' sacrifice for sin paid the debt originally incurred by Adam and took the punishment we deserved for our sins, a spiritual connection with God was once again made possible. All who accept Jesus' payment for their sins are reconciled to God.

Because every human being is a descendant of Adam, all are reckoned by God to be sinners "in Adam," and disqualified from having a relationship with God. Being "in Adam" means to be under the headship of Adam, the head of the human race, and part of Adam's family. Each person who places his faith in the Gospel of Christ is immediately credited with Christ's righteousness. God counts every believer to be righteous "in Christ," and transfers him from the

> For he hath made him to be sin for us, who knew no sin … (2 Cor 5:21a)

human family of Adam to the spiritual family of God. This transaction happens in the mind of God; it is not something we can see. Our new spiritual location is known as the Christian's position "in Christ," and the placing of us there is known as Holy Spirit baptism. The new spiritual entity created by this spiritual transaction is called "the body of Christ" and has Christ as its head instead of Adam (Ro 6:3; 1 Cor 12:13). Holy Spirit baptism is one of two spiritual transactions which occur when a person believes the Gospel. The other is regeneration, also known as being "born again," as explained earlier in this chapter.

Jesus died on a cross for the sins of mankind because all men are sinners who need a savior from God's wrath against sin. Jesus' death saves us because He paid both a physical and a spiritual price for sin, just as Adam did. He was a physical human substitute for mankind, replacing the first man, Adam, as the representative of the human race, and dying in our place for sin. He was also the object of God's wrath in the spiritual punishment for our sins, having been "made sin for us" (2 Cor 5:21). Having been declared guilty of the sins of the world, He was spiritually forsaken, separated from fellowship with the Father and the Holy Spirit while He hung on the cross (Mt 27:46b, Mk 15:31). Having a deeper understanding of the purpose and significance of Jesus' death can make it easier to explain to others exactly what Jesus did and why we need it.

Salvation from Sin is Accessed by Faith

Every person is a sinner who is in need of a savior from sin. Jesus Christ, God the Son, is that Savior, revealed in God's word, the Bible. We access salvation by believing the Gospel of Christ, found in 1 Corinthians 15:1-4.

Believing the Gospel is also known as having faith in it. To have faith means to be persuaded that something is true and, therefore, to trust in it (Ro 4:21; Heb 11:13). In describing the believer's relationship to God, Paul tells us, "It is by faith that it might be by grace" (Ro 4:16). The word "grace" can be translated as

> One cannot both receive a gift and work to earn it.

"undeserved favor," and receiving a favor is the opposite of working to earn something. Because one cannot both receive a gift and work to earn it, grace is contrasted with work. As an illustration, when I work, my employer is indebted to me, meaning I am owed wages for that work (Ro 4:4). The wages I earn are not a gift. However, when something is a gift of grace, it was not earned and not even deserved; it was just given.

It is important to note that there is no merit that I can claim for myself in recognizing what someone else has accomplished. Therefore, when I believe in what Christ did, I am not indebting God to me, as I would if I had earned what I received. Believing that the death, burial, and resurrection of Jesus Christ paid for my sins is a conviction; it has nothing whatsoever to do with my acumen, abilities, or achievements. In faith, I am looking away from myself to the work of another; I am trusting Him, and in what He did for me. Therefore, what I receive in return for my faith is gracious: I owe nothing for it. Because God loved me in Christ, in that spiritual transaction on the cross, He can freely give me the gift of salvation when I place my faith in the Gospel message (Ro 5:15-18, 6:23; Eph 2:8-9, Titus 3:5a). I am accepting what He did out of His love, and mercy, and goodness.

Any belief in works must be eliminated in order to accept the Gospel of Christ by faith. Just as it did in the garden, even one sin separates us from God and disqualifies us from earning salvation by good works. It is only by the faith system that God can provide salvation, so that it can be given as a free gift, by grace. It must be so, as no man could ever earn it.

Acts 13: A Real-Life Example of Witnessing

Although the Gospel contains necessary elements, because of the wide variety of beliefs among hearers, it cannot be used as a simple formula. A thorough understanding of its context and underlying truths enables Christians to answer questions and objections with confidence and clarity, explaining the "who, what, why, and how" of the Gospel, and defending the "where" if needed. When Paul shared the Gospel, it is unlikely that he simply recited the Gospel without offering any explanation. The most thorough record of Paul presenting the Gospel is found in Acts 13, where he is speaking to a group of Jews. If he had been speaking to Gentiles who didn't know the Old Testament scriptures, his explanation would likely have been slightly different, possibly excluding Israel's history, for example. All elements of the Gospel by which we are saved would have been presented to any audience, as well as answers to their questions. Because this passage from Acts 13 includes both the basics of the Gospel and many supporting truths behind those elements, it is worthy of careful study. We included verses 15-22 to provide context, then verses 23-44 with comments to identify the Gospel element that Paul is explaining.

> *15 And after the reading of the law and the prophets the rulers of the synagogue sent unto them, saying, Ye men and brethren, if ye have any word of exhortation for the people, say on. 16 Then Paul stood up, and beckoning with his hand said, Men of Israel, and ye that fear God, give audience. 17 The God of this people of Israel chose our fathers, and exalted the people when they dwelt as strangers in the land of Egypt, and with an high arm brought he them out of it. 18 And about the time of forty years suffered he their manners in the wilderness. 19 And when he had destroyed seven nations in the land of Canaan, he divided their land to them by lot. 20 And after that he gave unto them judges about the space of four hundred and fifty years, until Samuel the prophet. 21 And afterward they*

desired a king: and God gave unto them Saul the son of Cis,
a man of the tribe of Benjamin, by the space of forty years.
22 And when he had removed him, he raised up unto them
David to be their king; to whom also he gave testimony, and
said, I have found David the son of Jesse, a man after mine
own heart, which shall fulfil all my will.

23 Of this man's seed hath God
according to his promise raised unto
Israel a Saviour, Jesus: 24 When
John had first preached before his
coming the baptism of repentance
to all the people of Israel.

Jesus, the Savior, from the seed of David, as prophesied to Israel.

25 And as John fulfilled his course,
he said, Whom think ye that I am?
I am not he. But, behold, there
cometh one after me, whose shoes
of his feet I am not worthy to loose.
26 Men and brethren, children of the
stock of Abraham, and **whosoever**
among you feareth God, to you is
the word of this salvation sent.

This message is the saving message, available to all.

27 For they that dwell at Jerusalem,
and their rulers, because they
knew him not, nor yet the voices of
the prophets which are read every
sabbath day, they have fulfilled
them in condemning him.

28 And though they found no cause of death in him, yet desired they Pilate that he should be slain.

Jesus was an innocent substitute.

29 And when they had fulfilled all that was written of him, they took him down from the tree, and laid him in a sepulchre.

Jesus fulfilled all the prophecies about Him, according to the scriptures.

*30 But God raised him from the dead: 31 And he was seen many days of them which came up with him from Galilee to Jerusalem, who are his witnesses unto the people. 32 And we declare unto you **glad tidings,** how that the promise which was made unto the fathers, 33 God hath fulfilled the same unto us their children, in that he hath raised up Jesus again; as it is also written in the second psalm, Thou art my Son, this day have I begotten thee.*

This is the "good news," or gospel, that Jesus died on a tree, was buried and physically resurrected, all witnessed.

God kept His promises to the Jewish nation.

Jesus is God the Son, deity.

34 And as concerning that he raised him up from the dead, now no more to return to corruption, he said on this wise, I will give you the sure mercies of David.

*35 Wherefore he saith also in another psalm, Thou shalt not suffer thine **Holy One** to see corruption. 36 For David, after he had served his own generation by the will of God, fell on sleep, and was laid unto his fathers, and saw corruption: 37 But he, whom God raised again, saw no corruption.*

God's Old Testament title is used, connecting this "good news" with the Jewish prophecies. Jesus was sinless and could not be held by death.

*38 Be it known unto you therefore, men and brethren, that through **this man** is preached unto you the forgiveness of sins: 39 And by him all that believe are justified from all things, from which ye could not be justified by the law of Moses.*

Jesus is a real man. Forgiveness from sin is accessed by faith, not by law. Jesus' payment is sufficient for all sins, providing security to those who believe.

40 Beware therefore, lest that come upon you, which is spoken of in the prophets; 41 Behold, ye despisers, and wonder, and perish: for I work a work in your days, a work which ye shall in no wise believe, though a man declare it unto you. 42 And when the Jews were gone out of the synagogue, the Gentiles besought that these words might be preached to them the next sabbath.

*43 Now when the congregation was broken up, many of the Jews and religious proselytes followed Paul and Barnabas: who, speaking to them, **persuaded** them to continue in the grace of God. 44 And the next sabbath day came almost the whole city together to hear the word of God.* Acts 13:15-44

The will of man is moved by urging: persuasion was used to reason with the hearers about the truth of this message.

The Gospel of Christ is a Message

As important as what Paul's presentation contains, is what it does not contain. False versions of Christianity add to the Gospel works which negate grace. Noteworthy in Acts 13 is that only John's baptism of repentance for Israel is mentioned; water baptism for Christians is not mentioned, required, or practiced, nor is any other human effort, such as verbal declarations, promises to turn from sin, or requests to save. The Gospel of Christ is simply a message to be believed.

The fact that Paul gives a thorough explanation to his hearers does not mean that a person could not be saved by simply hearing the minimal elements of the Gospel, namely the death, burial, and resurrection of Jesus Christ for sin. The point is that as Christian witnesses we benefit no one by assuming that a hearer understands the Gospel's elements. What we hope to avoid in witnessing is a situation in which a person is presented an incomplete Gospel and fails to be saved because of a misunderstanding of its elements. As ministers of the Gospel, we believe there is no down-side to thoroughly understanding and explaining the who, what, why, how, and where of the Gospel of Christ, found in 1 Corinthians 15:1-4.

Can't I Just Tell People That Jesus Died for Their Sins?

This chapter detailing salvation is included because of our conviction as authors that many Christians make assumptions not only about the level of understanding of those to whom they witness, but also about the spiritual condition of friends and family, and even fellow church members. There is potential harm in assuming that a person is saved, or that he understands the meaning of the Gospel's elements, while a loving curiosity about the spiritual welfare of others and a willingness to discuss the Gospel is likely to provide many opportunities to glorify God through evangelism and discipleship.

If you have doubts about whether a complete and detailed explanation of the Gospel of Christ is important and necessary, here are some questions to ask yourself:

Could someone be saved if...

...he did not believe that Jesus is God?

...he believed that Jesus is not the only Savior of sinners and the only way to heaven?

...he believed that the source of the Gospel message, the Bible, is not God's word, but was written only by men?

...he thought that the Gospel was an allegory, and not a literal death, burial, and resurrection?

...he thought he was "not that bad" or a "good person" rather than a sinner?

...he denied that there is a price to be paid for sinning against God, who is holy and punishes sin?

...he believed that "making a commitment" in response to an altar call, getting baptized by water, "asking Jesus into his heart," or some other religious act saved him?

These questions exemplify commonly held beliefs of many who claim to believe the Gospel. We ask these questions earnestly to encourage Christians to eliminate unnecessary additions, popular shortcuts, and imprecise lingo from their evangelistic efforts, and instead simply explain the elements of 1 Corinthians 15:1-4. Shouldn't we, after all, take God at His word, and present the Gospel by which we are saved? What does it say about our own beliefs if we think we need to alter or "simplify" God's own message, which He calls the "good news" to mankind? Is there any reason to do so, if it could put to risk someone's eternal destiny? Because we care about the destiny of others, we need to share the exact message that God uses to save them.

The Gospel of Christ reveals who saved us, what He did, why we need it, how we get it, and the authority of where we find it. Since God included these facts within His saving message, we believe there is no justification for excluding, changing, or adding to any part of it. Lovingly explaining each element of the Gospel, and helping a hearer to understand its meaning, is the greatest blessing one person can bestow upon another.

T W O

WHO HE IS

God and the Person of Jesus Christ

The Gospel of Christ, found in 1 Corinthians 15:1-4, contains five elements which can be identified as who, what, why, how, and where. All five tell us something about Jesus Christ, God the Son.

- **Who:** Jesus is the one who died on a cross.
- **What:** He died as a sacrifice for sin.
- **Why:** Because every person is born in need of salvation from sin.
- **How:** Salvation is accessed by faith in His work on the cross for sins.
- **Where:** The authority and source of these truths is the Bible, the revelation of Jesus Christ to mankind.

Because Jesus' sacrifice on the cross is the object of our faith for salvation, who Jesus is must necessarily be central to the Gospel message. Objections to "who He is" may be in regard to Jesus in particular or to God in general, such as to God's triune nature, His attributes, or His character. Some take issue with Jesus' deity, considering Him a sort of "God-Junior," or merely a created being. Others do not recognize the differences between the God of the Bible and the deities of false religion, the movies, or their own imaginations.

Those who believe the record of the Bible know who God is. They believe the testimony of Israel's prophets, who proclaimed that God was their Savior. The New Testament identified to the world that God the Savior was the man Jesus of Nazareth. Believing in a

> Believing in a false Jesus does not save.

false God or a false Jesus does not save. This chapter responds to objections to who He is, a topic that is often part of the conversation when someone is asked a question about what he believes.

OBJECTION 1

"Jesus isn't God! He was just…" (a teacher, a prophet, a good man.)

A common objection to Jesus Christ is to deny that He is fully God, and one of the three divine persons who comprise the Godhead. Some consider Jesus a lesser being, a created being, or simply a man who was a moral teacher or a prophet. This is not the message of scripture, which reveals that Israel's Savior is God:

> Yet I am the LORD thy God from the land of Egypt, and thou shalt know no god but me: for there is no saviour beside me. (Hos 13:4)

John tells us that the Word, a title for Jesus Christ, is the Creator and is God:

In the beginning was the Word, and the Word was with God, and the Word was God. The same was in the beginning with God. All things were made by him; and without him was not any thing made that was made. (Jn 1:1-3)

Jesus' statement that He is one with the Father was a claim to be God. This was perfectly clear to the Jews, who were enraged by it:

> ... My Lord and my God. (Jn 20:28b)

I and my Father are one. Then the Jews took up stones again to stone him. Jesus answered them, Many good works have I shewed you from my Father; for which of those works do ye stone me? The Jews answered him, saying, For a good work we stone thee not; but for blasphemy; and because that thou, being a man, makest thyself God. (Jn 10:30-33)

Jesus did things that God would do. He performed miracles such as commanding the elements; He accepted worship, and He forgave sins:

And he saith unto them, Why are ye fearful, O ye of little faith? Then he arose, and rebuked the winds and the sea; and there was a great calm. But the men marvelled, saying, What manner of man is this, that even the winds and the sea obey him! (Mt 8:26-27)

And as they went to tell his disciples, behold, Jesus met them, saying, All hail. And they came and held him by the feet, and worshipped him. (Mt 28:9)

Whether is it easier to say to the sick of the palsy, Thy sins be forgiven thee; or to say, Arise, and take up thy bed, and walk? (Mk 2:9)

In addition to His words and deeds, Jesus' birth, ministry, and death fulfilled hundreds of biblical prophecies. Among them is one which calls his name Immanuel, meaning, "God with us."

> *Therefore the Lord himself shall give you a sign; Behold, a virgin shall conceive, and bear a son, and shall call his name Immanuel.* (Isa 7:14)

Colossians contains one of the most descriptive passages about the deity of Jesus Christ, describing Him as the Savior from sin, the very likeness of God, and the eternal Creator. Speaking of God the Father, and Jesus, who is God the Son, Paul writes:

> *Who hath delivered us from the power of darkness, and hath translated us into the kingdom of his dear Son: In whom we have redemption through his blood, even the forgiveness of sins: Who is the image of the invisible God, the firstborn of every creature: For by him were all things created, that are in heaven, and that are in earth, visible and invisible, whether they be thrones, or dominions, or principalities, or powers: all things were created by him, and for him: And he is before all things, and by him all things consist. And he is the head of the body, the church: who is the beginning, the firstborn from the dead; that in all things he might have the preeminence.* (Col 1:13-18)

Jesus declared Himself, "I am," a reference to His self-existent nature. This is the name God revealed to Moses:

> *And God said unto Moses, I AM THAT I AM: and he said, Thus shalt thou say unto the children of Israel, I AM hath sent me unto you.* (Ex 3:14)

That is why I told you that you will die in your sins, for unless you believe that I AM, you'll die in your sins. (Jn 8:24 ISV)

I'm telling you this now, before it happens, so that when it does happen, you may believe that I AM. (Jn 13:19 ISV)

Jesus said unto them, Verily, verily, I say unto you, Before Abraham was, I am. (Jn 8:58)

Jesus is a man, but He is not merely a man. The testimony of scripture is that Jesus is God the Son, the Creator, the I AM, and the fulfillment of the Old Testament prophecies that a savior would come.

OBJECTION 2

"God is not a trinity. The word isn't even in the Bible."

Although the word "trinity" is not in the Bible, it does describe a biblical concept. This doctrine is denied by many non-Christians, but there are probably few who are capable of raising a lucid objection to it. Similarly, it is likely that few Christians are able to defend the tri-unity of God by explaining it, so do not feel that you need to be a

> ... in the name of the Father, and the Son, and the Holy Ghost. (Mt 28:19b)

"Trinity expert" in order to effectively share the Gospel.

In your witnessing efforts, you may encounter some who are trained to refute the Trinity, and who can expertly draw you into a fruitless battle with this complex objection. Anti-trinitarian religions masquerading as Christian are willing to invest hours, and even weeks or months working toward the goal of converting a person to their belief. Sharing a few applicable verses will probably be sufficient to reveal whether or not the objector is willing to consider this doctrine.

Some denials of the Trinity are based on the claim that God is a singular entity who has three roles or forms. Such an explanation does not hold up when members of the Godhead make references to one another:

> *A little while, and ye shall not see me: and again, a little while, and ye shall see me, because I go to the Father.* (Jn 16:16)

> *But the Comforter, which is the Holy Ghost, whom the Father will send in my name, he shall teach you all things, and bring all things to your remembrance, whatsoever I have said unto you.* (Jn 14:26)

> *But when the Comforter is come, whom I will send unto you from the Father, even the Spirit of truth, which proceedeth from the Father, he shall testify of me…* (Jn 15:26)

> *And lo a voice from heaven, saying, This is my beloved Son, in whom I am well pleased.* (Mt 3:17)

Also supporting the doctrine of the Trinity are passages which make reference to all three persons in the Godhead:

Elect according to the foreknowledge of God the Father, through sanctification of the Spirit, unto obedience and sprinkling of the blood of Jesus Christ: Grace unto you, and peace, be multiplied. (1 Pet 1:2)

And be not drunk with wine, wherein is excess; but be filled with the Spirit; Speaking to yourselves in psalms and hymns and spiritual songs, singing and making melody in your heart to the Lord; Giving thanks always for all things unto God and the Father in the name of our Lord Jesus Christ. (Eph 5:18-20)

For through him we both have access by one Spirit unto the Father. (Eph 2:18)

Come ye near unto me, hear ye this; I have not spoken in secret from the beginning; from the time that it was, there am I: and now the Lord GOD, and his Spirit, hath sent me. Thus saith the LORD, thy Redeemer, the Holy One of Israel; I am the LORD thy God which teacheth thee to profit, which leadeth thee by the way that thou shouldest go. (Isa 48:16-17)

For unto us a child is born, unto us a son is given: and the government shall be upon his shoulder: and his name shall be called Wonderful, Counsellor, The mighty God, The everlasting Father, The Prince of Peace. (Isa 9:6)

A subtle revelation of the Trinity can be found in the biblical use of pronouns, such as in Genesis Chapter 1. When Moses refers to God, he uses the singular words "his" and "he." When describing the persons of God communicating amongst themselves, the plural "us" is used:

*And God said, Let **us** make man in **our** image, after **our**
likeness: and let them have dominion over the fish of the sea,
and over the fowl of the air, and over the cattle, and over all
the earth, and over every creeping thing that creepeth upon
the earth. So God created man in **his** own image, in the image
of God created **he** him; male and female created **he** them."*
(Gen 1:26-27)

It is difficult to describe the Trinity because there is nothing and
no one else like God, but it can help to compare Him to something
we understand, such as humankind. We will refer to the kind of
being that God is as "God-kind."

There is only one being that can be classified as God-kind; there
is no other like Him. If we compare the substance of God-kind
with that of humankind, we know that humankind exists in
an individual human body which is made of matter. God-kind,
however, is spirit. Spirit is what He is made of; it is the substance
of His being.

God reveals Himself as being one and also as existing in three
persons. When God is described as being one, it means that He
is one spirit, the only one of His kind. God-kind is also a trinity,
referring to the fact that three persons share one spirit. The persons
of God are not separate individuals as are humans, who exist
independently from one another. God is unique: one God in three
persons.

The unity of God, meaning that God is one spirit, is taught in
scripture:

*And Jesus answered him, The first of all the commandments
is, Hear, O Israel; The Lord our God is one Lord...* (Mk 12:29)

Thou believest that there is one God; thou doest well: the devils also believe, and tremble. (Jas 2:19)

God is Spirit: and those who worship him must worship in spirit and truth. (Jn 4:24 NSAB)

Additional support for the Trinity is that all three divine persons are called "God." The Father is God:

Blessed be God, even the Father of our Lord Jesus Christ, the Father of mercies, and the God of all comfort. (2 Cor 1:3)

And that every tongue should confess that Jesus Christ is Lord, to the glory of God the Father. (Phil 2:11)

The second person of the Trinity, the Son, is God:

In the beginning was the Word, and the Word was with God, and the Word was God. (Jn 1:1)

For in him dwelleth all the fullness of the Godhead bodily. (Col 2:9)

The third person of the Trinity, the Holy Spirit, is God:

But Peter said, Ananias, why hath Satan filled thine heart to lie to the Holy Ghost, and to keep back part of the price of the land? Whiles it remained, was it not thine own? and after it was sold, was it not in thine own power? why hast thou conceived this thing in thine heart? thou hast not lied unto men, but unto God. (Acts 5:3-4)

The Spirit of the Lord spake by me, and his word was in my tongue. (2 Sam 23:2)

Any one of the aforementioned aspects of God or several of them might be needed to answer the questions of hearers about God. As witnesses of the Gospel of Christ, we can allow the Bible to speak for itself to describe Him. Doing so allows each hearer to decide for himself if he believes the biblical record.

OBJECTION 3

"The Bible has two different gods: an angry, punitive god in the Old Testament, and a kind and forgiving Jesus in the New Testament. These cannot be the same God, so I don't believe."

Using an unbalanced portrayal of God in the Bible, some objectors claim that the God described in the Old Testament is different than Jesus. Seeming differences, however, only reflect the various aspects of God's character shown throughout scripture. That God is not one-dimensional is apparent when the

> For I am the LORD, I change not...
> (Mal 3:6a)

whole counsel of scripture is considered. In an attempt to distinguish Jesus in the New Testament from God in the Old Testament, objectors characterize Him as passive and mild, but He sometimes expressed righteous anger:

> *And they come to Jerusalem: and Jesus went into the temple, and began to cast out them that sold and bought in the temple, and overthrew the tables of the moneychangers, and the seats of them that sold doves; And would not suffer that*

any man should carry any vessel through the temple. And he
taught, saying unto them, Is it not written, My house shall be
called of all nations the house of prayer? But ye have made it a
den of thieves! (Mk 11:15-17)

Selectively using Old Testament verses, objectors accuse God of
being angry and punitive. On the contrary, His dealings with
Adam and Eve, those of Noah's time, the people of Ninevah, and
rebellious Israel belie this characterization. Psalm 145 contains one
of many beautiful Old Testament tributes to God's character amid
the repeated failings of His chosen nation Israel:

The LORD is gracious, and full of compassion; slow to anger,
and of great mercy. The LORD is good to all: and his tender
mercies are over all his works. (Ps 145:8-9)

God's character is perfectly balanced. He is kind, loving, patient,
and merciful toward mankind. He is also just and always does
rightly, which includes dispensing just punishment. Because God
is teaching mankind different lessons at various times in history,
some Bible portions put a greater emphasis on a particular aspect
of God's character. An example of one of God's lessons to humanity
is that He is holy and we are sinful. Referring to the Law of Moses,
Paul explains God's purpose in administering Israel with a legal
system:

Therefore by the deeds of the law there shall no flesh be
justified in his sight: for by the law is the knowledge of sin.
(Ro 3:20)

Under God's perfect law system, the failings of man were made
clear, thereby displaying the holiness of God in contrast. Providing
evidence that humanity is sinful was meant to illuminate man's

need for a savior. When the Savior came, John tells us that Jesus' ministry had a different purpose than did the Law:

> For the law was given by Moses, but grace and truth came by
> Jesus Christ. (Jn 1:17)

Jesus' ministry was to display God's grace, culminating in His death on a cross to pay for the sins of the world. In the New Testament, we do not see a different god, or a change in God; what we see is a new chapter in God's plan and a new administration over His people. For Christians, recognizing the unfolding revelation within the Bible is crucial to both rightly understanding it and explaining it to hearers. Those who believe that the Bible contradicts itself in describing who God is can be shown His unfolding plan and the various facets of His holy character.

OBJECTION 4

"God is love, and a loving God would not send anyone to hell."

In some cases, an objection to who God is, is due to a misunderstanding of His good character. Denying the consequence of sin is an example of this because it denies God's holiness. Objecting to hell by protesting that "God is love" misses the point that failing to judge sin is the equivalent of approving of it. Yes, God is love, but He is also just, always acting rightly. A human judge who let a convicted murderer go unpunished would not be considered to be performing an act of love, but one of corruption for failing to dispense justice. Because God's character is balanced between His loving kindness and His holy justice, He cannot ignore sin. Therefore, He has provided a

> And in hell he lift up his eyes, being in torment... (Lk 16:23a)

solution to the problem of sin which is free, available to all, and recorded in the Gospel of Christ, 1 Corinthians 15:1-4. An objector who believes in a one-sided god does not believe in the righteous God of the Bible.

God's holiness was on display under the Law of Moses, which clearly and continually revealed God's high expectations and the sinful failings of mankind:

> *And Joshua said unto the people, Ye cannot serve the LORD: for he is an holy God; he is a jealous God; he will not forgive your transgressions nor your sins. If ye forsake the LORD, and serve strange gods, then he will turn and do you hurt, and consume you, after that he hath done you good.* (Josh 24:19-20)

> *Sanctify yourselves therefore, and be ye holy: for I am the LORD your God. And ye shall keep my statutes, and do them: I am the LORD which sanctify you.* (Lev 20:7-8)

God asked His people to act in accordance with His holiness, but their disobedience revealed the need for a savior from sin. In the New Testament, the Savior was provided, and God's grace was displayed:

And the Word was made flesh, and dwelt among us, (and we beheld his glory, the glory as of the only begotten of the Father,) full of grace and truth (Jn 1:14)

For the law was given by Moses, but grace and truth came by Jesus Christ. (Jn 1:17)

If we confess our sins, he is faithful and just to forgive us our sins, and to cleanse us from all unrighteousness. (1 Jn 1:9)

The Gospel shows God's provision to satisfy both His holiness and His love for mankind. His holiness was satisfied by pouring out the punishment for sin upon a substitute for mankind, the person of Jesus Christ. God's love was satisfied by offering to all mankind a payment for sins, a gift which is available through faith in the death, burial, and resurrection of Jesus Christ. Perhaps the hearer who objects to hell has not considered that he is counting his own mercy and judgment to be superior to God's, or that he is attacking the record of the Bible and the honesty of Jesus, who spoke of hell many times and died to save us from it. Jesus is God in the flesh. He was not misinformed or lying when he warned his listeners of judgment to come:

And if thy right hand offend thee, cut it off, and cast it from thee: for it is profitable for thee that one of thy members should perish, and not that thy whole body should be cast into hell. (Mt 5:30)

Ye serpents, ye generation of vipers, how can ye escape the damnation of hell? (Mt 23:33)

Because of who He is, God will ultimately provide justice for all. Because of God's love and mercy, He has also provided a solution to the problem of sin. His desire is that none should perish but rather that all should come to repentance (2 Pet 3:9). As Christian witnesses, we can help hearers to recognize that hell is the selection that each person makes for himself when he rejects the provision of God for his eternal destiny.

OBJECTION 5

"There is too much suffering and evil in the world. I reject a God who allows it!"

A hearer who objects to the Gospel because of the world's suffering is not seeing God as good, perhaps because of painful losses of his own. Gently inquiring about whether that is the case can be a good place to start. Without the biblical perspective to reveal the "big picture" of life, this world might seem to offer little more than pain, disappointment, and only fleeting happiness. As Christians, we have a hope beyond this world

> ... be of good cheer; I have overcome the world. (Jn 16:33b)

which is a comfort to us. Those who see no solution to the world's troubles sometimes see God as heartless, and Christians as escapists who only want to dream of heaven and not fix the problems here. They do not yet understand that believing the Gospel *is* the solution, by freeing us from sin and death. As we share who God is, a hearer may be willing to consider the Bible's response to suffering.

To explain suffering and evil, a Christian witness would do well to include its cause, beginning with the fall of Adam and Eve, covered in Chapter One of this book. The objection, however, is really an expression of doubt regarding God's goodness. God is the easy target of blame for the world's troubles, but He is not the cause. Suffering did not exist when God created the earth; what He created was good:

> *And God saw everything that he had made, and, behold, it was very good.* (Gen 1:31a)

Our good God not only provides for His children; He even provides for those who reject Him:

> *That ye may be the children of your Father which is in heaven: for he maketh his sun to rise on the evil and on the good, and sendeth rain on the just and on the unjust.* (Mt 5:45)

God helps His children when asked. He offers a moral code that, when followed, allows us to avoid many calamities. He fulfills prophecy so that we know He always keeps His word.

> *And this is the confidence that we have in him, that, if we ask any thing according to his will, he heareth us...* (1 Jn 5:14)

> *And we know that all things work together for good to them that love God, to them who are the called according to his purpose.* (Ro 8:28)

> *For whatsoever things were written aforetime were written for our learning, that we through patience and comfort of the scriptures might have hope.* (Ro 15:4)

Some of the earth's problems are due to the curse of sin. God did curse the earth (Gen 3:17-19), but He also provided a solution to sin and a future free from its evils:

> *And God shall wipe away all tears from their eyes; and there shall be no more death, neither sorrow, nor crying, neither shall there be any more pain: for the former things are passed away.* (Rev 21:4)

The earth is sin-cursed because the first two people rejected God's wise counsel. Therefore, even the problems that are not directly caused by man today were indirectly caused by man. It was Adam who sinned, and we would all do the same; we would act independently from God and disobey Him, because everyone who is less than God will act less

> Everyone who is less than God will act less than godly.

than godly. Much of this world's suffering continues to be caused by man, and is done in opposition to God's will:

> *And GOD saw that the wickedness of man was great in the earth, and that every imagination of the thoughts of his heart was only evil continually. And it repented the LORD that he had made man on the earth, and it grieved him at his heart.* (Gen 6:5-6)

Humanity is fallen and sinful, perpetrating many evils. It can be frustrating when things seem unfair, but God is just, and nobody will "get away" with anything:

> *Dearly beloved, avenge not yourselves, but rather give place unto wrath: for it is written, Vengeance is mine; I will repay, saith the Lord.* (Ro 12:19)

The issue of suffering returns us to the matter of God's character, and specifically to whether or not He is good. The evidence that He is good can be seen in the hope He offers for our future. The biblical meaning of hope is to have a confident expectation:

In hope of eternal life, which God, that cannot lie, promised before the world began. (Titus 1:2)

But I would not have you to be ignorant, brethren, concerning them which are asleep, that ye sorrow not, even as others which have no hope. (1 Thes 4:13)

Now the God of hope fill you with all joy and peace in believing, that ye may abound in hope, through the power of the Holy Ghost. (Ro 15:13)

For God sent not his Son into the world to condemn the world; but that the world through him might be saved. (Jn 3:17)

Blessed be the God and Father of our Lord Jesus Christ, which according to his abundant mercy hath begotten us again unto a lively hope by the resurrection of Jesus Christ from the dead... (1 Pet 1:3)

Wherefore gird up the loins of your mind, be sober, and hope to the end for the grace that is to be brought unto you at the revelation of Jesus Christ... (1 Pet 1:13)

If we look away from the calamities of this world and acknowledge that much of what happens in this life is not according to God's will, we can place our confident expectation in Him. God's word tells us who He is, assuring a perfect eternity to all who believe Him. Yes, there is suffering in the world, but by believing the Gospel of Christ, we have surety and hope for our future (1 Cor 15:1-4). It is this message that we wish to convey to hearers who object to God because they blame Him for the world's suffering.

OBJECTION 6

"I believe in...
> ...something like the 'Star Wars force' with a dark and light side."
> ...the god of my own understanding."
> ...some kind of higher power."
> ...well, not the God of the Bible."

Considering the wide variety of ideas about who God is, it is not surprising that Jesus said many people will believe anything *except* the truth:

> And **because** I tell you the truth, ye believe me not. (Jn 8:45)

An impersonal force that can be used to accomplish things is a popular idea about who God is. The "Star Wars force," for example, can be used for good or evil, depending upon who wields it. Nature is a kind of god to some, but nature has no personality; you can't have a relationship with forces of nature. Tribal gods are unpredictable and untrustworthy. Mohammed, the founder of Islam, made his tribal god, Allah, the god of a new religion.

> For in him dwelleth all the fullness of the Godhead bodily. (Col 2:9)

But Allah has no concern for his followers. He is distant, unjust and not at all merciful. His followers cannot count on him and never know what to expect from him. The God of the Bible is both personal and concerned for all mankind.

Despite the differences among various religions regarding who God is, they all teach some standard of behavior or have rules to follow. With a standard comes the need for a judge who must determine if followers meet the standard. But only a personal God can be a judge; neither nature nor a "force" can make moral determinations. Only a person has a conscience and can know right from wrong. The God of the Bible is more than a judge; He is a righteous judge. He calls us to use reason and to display virtue. The scriptures testify that the character of the true God, Jehovah, is goodness and love, kindness and grace, reason and justice, help and hope. He is a personal God, and we can know Him, trust Him, and have a relationship with Him:

> *And I will give them an heart to know me, that I am the LORD: and they shall be my people, and I will be their God: for they shall return unto me with their whole heart. (Jer 24:7)*

> *But let him that glorieth glory in this, that he understandeth and knoweth me, that I am the LORD which exercise lovingkindness, judgment, and righteousness, in the earth: for in these things I delight, saith the LORD. (Jer 9:24)*

> *Behold, we count them happy which endure. Ye have heard of the patience of Job, and have seen the end of the Lord; that the Lord is very pitiful, and of tender mercy. (Jas 5:11)*

This then is the message which we have heard of him, and declare unto you, that God is light, and in him is no darkness at all. (1 Jn 1:5)

God is personal and of upright character. He cares about His children, offering us security and assurance of our future:

These things have I written unto you that believe on the name of the Son of God; that ye may know that ye have eternal life, and that ye may believe on the name of the Son of God. (1 Jn 5:13)

Unlike an impersonal force, or a capricious counterfeit deity, our all-powerful God knows the future, is involved in it, and brings about the outcomes He desires:

I'm telling you this now, before it happens, so that when it does happen, you may believe that I AM. (Jn 13:19 ISV)

Behold, I am the LORD, the God of all flesh: is there anything too hard for me? (Jer 32:27)

Declaring the end from the beginning, and from ancient times the things that are not yet done, saying, My counsel shall stand, and I will do all my pleasure… (Isa 46:10)

For I am the LORD: I will speak, and the word that I shall speak shall come to pass; it shall be no more prolonged: for in your days, O rebellious house, will I say the word, and will perform it, saith the Lord GOD. (Ezek 12:25)

The God of the Bible is not only personal; He is unique because He has always existed. He declares that He is the only God:

Before the mountains were brought forth, or ever thou hadst formed the earth and the world, even from everlasting to everlasting, thou art God. (Ps 90:2)

Ye are my witnesses, saith the LORD, and my servant
whom I have chosen: that ye may know and believe me, and
understand that I am he: before me there was no God formed,
neither shall there be after me. I, even I, am the LORD; and
beside me there is no saviour. I have declared, and have saved,
and I have shewed, when there was no strange god among
you: therefore ye are my witnesses saith the LORD, that I am
God. Yea, before the day was I am he; and there is none that
can deliver out of my hand: I will work, and who shall let it?
(Isa 43:10-13)

A force, lacking personhood, cannot give the world spiritual concepts such as beauty, liberty, or love. The competing gods of the false religions cannot prove themselves to be the one true God. The God of the Bible is the one and only Creator:

Thus saith the LORD, thy redeemer, and he that formed thee
from the womb, I am the LORD that maketh all things; that
stretcheth forth the heavens alone; that spreadeth abroad the
earth by myself... (Isa 44:24)

I have made the earth, and created man upon it: I, even my
hands, have stretched out the heavens, and all their host have
I commanded. (Isa 45:12)

For thus saith the LORD that created the heavens; God
himself that formed the earth and made it; he hath established
it, he created it not in vain, he formed it to be inhabited: I am
the LORD; and there is none else. (Isa 45:18)

Because of the multitude of false religions, the objections to who God is can be complex, so a simple response to this objection might be best. Asking the hearer if he is willing to explain his disbelief in the biblical God may reveal that he has no concrete reason for denying who God is. If he does have a reason, another simple question may suffice, such as asking him what evidence he has of his conviction. He may have faulty "evidence" or none at all, and allowing him to realize this for

> Unto thee it was shewed, that thou mightest know that the LORD he is God; there is none else beside him. (Deut 4:35)

himself might be more effective than trying to convince him. A question such as, "Are you absolutely certain about your eternal destiny?" can be much more powerful than any argument or explanation. Strange ideas are endless, but God offers proof of who He is. This provides security and peace to those who believe; and for those who are willing to hear the testimony of His word, the evidence is worthy of consideration.

Considering who God is, one of the most wonderful things about Him is that He lets us know that He understands us. He isn't looking to pounce every time we fail. He knows we are frail, and weak, and that we need His tender mercy:

> *The LORD is merciful and gracious, slow to anger, and plenteous in mercy. He will not always chide: neither will he keep his anger for ever. He hath not dealt with us after our sins; nor rewarded us according to our iniquities. For as the heaven is high above the earth, so great is his mercy toward them that fear him. As far as the east is from the west, so far hath he removed our transgressions from us. Like as a father pitieth his children, so the LORD pitieth them that fear him. For he knoweth our frame; he remembereth that we are dust.* (Ps 103:8-14)

Unlike the elements of the earth, or some kind of "force," or a distant, unknowable god, our God saves. No religion in the world or in history can say the same. In every way He is a good God, an important truth to convey to those who are willing to hear who He really is.

> *That at the name of Jesus every knee should bow, of things in heaven, and things in earth, and things under the earth; And that every tongue should confess that Jesus Christ is Lord, to the glory of God the Father.* (Phil 2:10-11)

_____

_____

_____

T H R E E

WHAT HE DID

Death, Burial, and Resurrection for Sin

Whether Christians ask someone a question about their faith, we hope to be able to discuss what Jesus did. Jesus Christ died on a cross as a sacrifice for sins. There are many objections to what He did, and the most common by far is the idea that His sacrifice is not sufficient to save. An insufficient sin payment requires that law-keeping or good works be added to the work of Christ, a belief commonly referred to as "legalism." Such objections are closely related to the topic of Chapter 6, which addresses faith alone for salvation. Whether an objector to "what He did" mixes law with grace, or presents some other objection, his disbelief in the death, burial, and resurrection of Jesus Christ as a completed payment for sin is a rejection of the Gospel of Christ, found in 1 Corinthians 15:1-4.

It Didn't Happen?

The Bible contains the detailed historical record of the death, burial, and resurrection of Jesus Christ, including the fact that there were hundreds of witnesses to the event. Although Christians know that the resurrection is a documented event of ancient history, deniers exist. For example, a Muslim or a Jew may deny the resurrection of Jesus because both Islam and modern, non-biblical Judaism dispute the historical record. In the first case, Islam teaches that Jesus was not crucified:

> "That they said (in boast), 'We killed Christ Jesus the son of Mary, the Messenger of Allah';—but they killed him not, nor crucified him, but so it was made to appear to them, and those who differ therein are full of doubts, with no (certain) knowledge, but only conjecture to follow, for of a surety they killed him not." (Koran, Sura 4:157)

Similarly, Judaism denies the resurrection of Christ and does not accept Him as its prophesied savior. The Bible testifies that in an effort to cover up His resurrection, the chief priests and elders of Israel bribed the Roman guards to lie about the disappearance of Jesus' body:

> Allah denies the crucifixion. He is not Jehovah.

> *And when they were assembled with the elders, and had taken counsel, they gave large money unto the soldiers, Saying, Say ye, His disciples came by night, and stole him away while we slept. And if this come to the governor's ears, we will persuade him, and secure you. So they took the money, and did as they were taught: and this saying is commonly reported among the Jews until this day.* (Mt 28:12-15)

It Happened, But...

Even those who assent to the biblical record of history and its testimony of Jesus' sacrifice may object to the sufficiency of Jesus' payment for sin. Some objections are easily-detected lists of "do's" to get saved and "don'ts" to avoid the lake of fire. Others are more subtle, manifesting themselves in doubts about the surety of forgiveness or of faith alone to receive it. Learning that someone believes that works are necessary for salvation, or that morality is what makes someone a Christian, could be that

> Denying the sufficiency of the Gospel is a rejection of it.

uncomfortable moment when you realize that the person next to you in the church pew is the one who needs to hear the Gospel.

The belief that something needs to be added to the death, burial, and resurrection of Jesus Christ for sin is a rejection of Him as a satisfactory sacrifice. Here are some variations of denying the sufficiency of the cross:

- "You have to be good." Some sins are so bad or some people are so evil that they are disqualified from heaven, but most people are not, and will get to heaven. Believing that man can be good, this objector denies the inherent sinfulness of man and nullifies Christ's payment for the sins of the world, replacing it with human morality.

- "I need faith and..." Believing alone is not sufficient to receive the payment for sin; we must do something also. Salvation amounts to a partnership between Jesus and me as co-redeemers, in which we both contribute something to salvation. This is often a plainly-stated denial, such as a belief in the necessity of a church ritual.

- "Some of the Law is still in effect." Certain works must be done or laws obeyed to qualify for heaven. The practical object of faith is the works or laws. A common example is believing that it is possible to keep the 10 commandments.

These are all forms of legalism, also called law-keeping, law-works, or works salvation. Legalism is a misunderstanding or denial of the gracious nature of salvation, and its variations are merely differences in what is emphasized. Whether some activity must be avoided or some merit added in order to gain salvation, legalism is a rejection of the Gospel of Christ. Determining the particular nature of the objection will help in your response. An easy example to use when trying to determine if a person believes in the sufficiency of Christ's sacrifice for sin is the universally agreed upon most-evil-person-ever...

OBJECTION 7

"So you think anyone can go to heaven? Even Hitler?!"

Comparison is at the heart of human achievement; we evaluate our efforts by comparing them to those of others. But salvation is not an achievement; it is a gracious gift. We gain something in salvation that we do not deserve, simply by faith in what someone else accomplished on our behalf. Our unworthiness for heaven is not in comparison to others, but in comparison to the perfect holiness of God.

> For there is no respect of persons with God. (Ro 2:11)

Faith is the perfect way to access God's grace for salvation because it excludes any kind of human effort. Mighty or weak, genius or average, pious or fallen, we are all able to receive forgiveness of sins... even Hitler. It may seem unfair that an evil person has the same opportunity for salvation as a sweet grandmother, but if fairness was the standard, we would all be in the lake of fire. God has no "respect of persons," meaning He deals with all men justly, and without bias, even including Hitler (Ro 2:11, Acts 10:34, Eph 6:9, Col 3:25).

Some hearers think too well of humanity (excepting Hitler) and misunderstand human nature. A common refrain is, "People are basically good." This contradicts the biblical declaration that we are all born sinners, in need of salvation from sin, and in possession of nothing worthy of God. Children are a familiar example of this; they do not need to be taught to hit their siblings, hoard their toys, or say, "No!" to Mommy. The assessment of our condition as sinners is not from our point of view, but from the perfect and holy perspective of our Creator, as expressed by King David:

> Behold, I was shapen in iniquity; and in sin did my mother conceive me. (Ps 51:5)

Those who trust in their good works think that they have something of value to offer God. But God excludes human effort for salvation, proclaiming that even our "righteousnesses,"—our very *best* works—are filthy and tainted with sin:

> But we are all as an unclean thing, and all our righteousnesses are as filthy rags; and we all do fade as a leaf; and our iniquities, like the wind, have taken us away. (Isaiah 64:6)

Upon understanding God's evaluation of our human efforts, we dare not offer Him the dirty rags of our works, but can only fall before Him in need of His mercy to save us. If one believes that all of us "good people" are qualified for heaven, while Hitler and a few others are not, then human merit is a factor in salvation. Such a view can only render the death, burial, and resurrection of Jesus

Christ insufficient to save. Making no meritorious distinctions among men, God's word declares that Jesus Christ died for the sins of the whole world:

> And he is the propitiation for our sins: and not for ours only, but also **for the** sins **of** **the whole world**. (1 Jn 2:2)

> **For God so loved the world**, that he gave his only begotten Son, that whosoever believeth in him should not perish, but have everlasting life. For God sent not his Son into the world to condemn the world; but **that the world through him might be saved**. (Jn 3:16-17)

> And said unto the woman, Now we believe, not because of thy saying: for we have heard him ourselves, and know that this is indeed the Christ, **the Saviour of the world**. (Jn 4:42)

> I am the living bread which came down from heaven: if any man eat of this bread, he shall live for ever: and the bread that I will give is my flesh, which **I will give for the life of the world**. (Jn 6:51)

> To wit, that God was in Christ, **reconciling the world** unto himself, not imputing their trespasses unto them; and hath committed unto us the word of reconciliation. (2 Cor 5:19)

Because many will reject the payment for their sins, the whole world will not be in heaven. But all those who believed the Gospel of Christ for salvation will be there.

_____

_____

_____

"Yes, I believe the gospel, but I still need to do my share."

Some who object to what Jesus did, do so indirectly. Such an objector might agree that there is a universal need for salvation, that mankind is sinful, and that God is just in requiring a penalty for sin. Even so, misunderstanding that Christians are called to do good works *after* salvation is what leads him away from the sufficiency of the cross. Because God allows Christians to share in His work here on earth, this objector sees no rejection of grace in "doing his part" in salvation as well. The partnership in ministry between God and His people is misapplied, and is, therefore, thought to help secure salvation. Our partnership with God, however, is only after we are cleansed by the blood of Christ.

Although it is unlikely that anyone would consider himself a co-redeemer, this is the unavoidable conclusion if he must contribute to his own salvation. The objector who cannot believe that there is nothing we can do to be saved can be shown the testimony of scripture. In many places it teaches that we are to simply believe in order to receive this gift:

> *And whosoever liveth and believeth in me shall never die. Believest thou this?* (Jn 11:26)

> *To him give all the prophets witness, that through his name whosoever believeth in him shall receive remission of sins.* (Acts 10:43)

> *For the wages of sin is death; but the gift of God is eternal life through Jesus Christ our Lord.* (Ro 6:23)

*But God, who is rich in mercy, for his great love wherewith he loved us, Even when we were dead in sins, hath quickened us together with Christ, (by grace ye are saved;) And hath raised us up together, and made us sit together in heavenly places in Christ Jesus: That in the ages to come he might shew the exceeding riches of his grace in his kindness toward us through Christ Jesus. For by grace are ye saved through faith; and that not of yourselves: it is the **gift** of God: **Not of works**, lest any man should boast.* (Eph 2:4-9)

OBJECTION 9

"So you just throw out part of the Bible? I believe all of it!"

Many objections to the death, burial, and resurrection of Jesus Christ for sin are made because the objector does not believe that His sacrifice can save without the addition of something else. Often what is added is Old Testament law. This objector believes the Bible, and therefore thinks that all of it is currently applicable. He does not distinguish between the administration of the Nation of Israel by law, and the church by the principle of grace. Failing to make a distinction between the Old and New Testaments is a common source of legalism.

All of the Bible is for believers, but not all of it is to us. In describing creation, Israel's history, God's character, fulfilled prophecy, and future events, the Old Testament's role today is summarized by Paul:

> *For whatsoever things were written aforetime were written for our learning, that we through patience and comfort of the scriptures might have hope.* (Ro 15:4)

The church can learn from the Law, but it is not to operate by law. Numerous Bible verses specifically exclude law-works both for initial salvation and for Christian living. Adherence to a works or law system is a rejection of the gracious gift of salvation. God is not impressed with our works; He is impressed with the work of the Son. Anyone who rejects the payment of Jesus Christ for his sins will spend eternity in the lake of fire, paying for his own sins (Rev 20:14-15).

> God is not impressed with our works; He is impressed with the work of the Son.

If law-works are needed for salvation, then Jesus' sacrificial death did not fully pay for sin. But we know that His payment was sufficient and accepted by God. After Jesus died, He descended into "the lower parts of the earth" (Eph 4:9, 1 Pet 3:19). He did not remain there, however, but returned from the dead. The debt owed on every sin had already been paid on the cross. That is why Jesus proclaimed, "It is finished" (Jn 19:30).

> *Whom God hath raised up, having loosed the pains of death: because it was not possible that he should be holden of it.* (Acts 2:24)

He seeing this before spake of the resurrection of Christ,
that his soul was not left in hell, neither his flesh did see
corruption. (Acts 2:31)

A relatable example of a payment made in full is that when I have paid off my car loan, that debt is gone. If Jesus pays my sin debt, it's gone too. But, if I am doing works to please, appease, or pay God, I am in fact offering those works as a payment for my sins, instead of accepting the free gift of salvation. It cannot be both. Either something is a free gift, or it is worked for and earned or purchased. Any payment makes an item received no longer a gift. Believing that the salvation purchased by Christ must be gained or earned by the sinner means that either the gift has been rejected, or the offer has not been understood.

No Defense for Law

The charge that Christians have thrown out the Old Testament is serious and deserves additional attention. It is not a rejection of the Old Testament to believe that Jesus' death paid for all sin without the works of the Law. The Old Testament law and prophets made obvious man's need for a savior, and identified Him when He arrived. Testifying to the love, faithfulness, and longsuffering of God as He dealt with His chosen nation, Israel, the Old Testament is instructive and comforting to Christians (Ro 15:4).

Efforts to be obedient to law are exceedingly common among many who call themselves Christians. Law-keeping can take as many forms as people have ideas for trying to impress God. Some are personal, while others are denominational, attached to a certain type of church. Some are unique, and others are variations of Old Testament law. Trying to incorporate Old Testament law into the grace system of the church is the most widely used form of law-works, and is our focus here.

There are several reasons why Old Testament law-keeping cannot be part of salvation:

- Adding law-keeping to salvation is a denial of the sufficiency of Christ's sacrifice for sin.
- It is impossible for any man to keep even a fraction of the Law.
- The Law was never intended to save. Its purpose was to reveal sin, and to show those who lived under it their need for a savior.

The Law had 613 requirements; nobody can even keep the most well-known 10. The same would be true for any law system; no matter what rules a person sets for himself, eventually he will break them. The Old Testament Law of Moses, or Mosaic Law, expressed God's *perfect* standard. Therefore, any lesser level of performance in an effort to gain salvation has already fallen short. No person other than Jesus Christ has ever perfectly kept the Law, so if it is needed for entrance into heaven, nobody is getting in.

> *For neither they themselves who are circumcised keep the law; but desire to have you circumcised, that they may glory in your flesh.* (Gal 6:13)

Now therefore why tempt ye God, to put a yoke upon the neck of the disciples, which neither our fathers nor we were able to bear? (Acts 15:10)

Laws of any kind do nothing more than inform a lawbreaker of his violation; they cannot deliver the lawbreaker from its penalty. For example, if I drive past a 35 mph speed limit sign while driving 55, it shows me that I am guilty. Obeying the law in the future does not change the fact that I broke it in the past, nor exonerate me from the consequences. The letters to the church make it perfectly clear that the Law is not part of initial salvation nor the perfecting purpose of the Christian walk.

> *But now **we are delivered from the law**, that being dead wherein we were held; that we should serve in newness of spirit, and not in the oldness of the letter. What shall we say then? Is the law sin? God forbid. Nay, **I had not known sin, but by the law**: for I had not known lust, except the law had said, Thou shalt not covet.* (Ro 7:6-7)

> *For **the law made nothing perfect**, but the bringing in of a better hope did; by the which we draw nigh unto God.* (Heb 7:19)

> *For **the law** having a shadow of good things to come, and not the very image of the things, **can never with those sacrifices** which they offered year by year continually **make the comers thereunto perfect**.* (Heb 10:1)

> *Wherefore the law was our schoolmaster to bring us unto Christ, that we might be justified by faith. But **after that faith is come, we are no longer under a schoolmaster**.* (Gal 3:24-25)

*For **what the law could not do,** in that it was weak through the flesh, God sending his own Son in the likeness of sinful flesh, and for sin, condemned sin in the flesh...* (Ro 8:3)

For those who have the righteousness of Christ, the Law serves no purpose. Powerless to remedy or undo the fact that it has been violated, the Law is only a revealer of sin, and not a solution to it. Only by God's grace can sin be forgiven. Law, in fact, "frustrates" grace, making Christ's victory over sin of no effect:

I do not frustrate the grace of God: for if righteousness come by the law, then Christ is dead in vain. (Gal 2:21)

For I through the law am dead to the law, that I might live unto God. (Gal 2:19)

The reason that law frustrates grace is because one must reject gracious salvation in order to instead work to earn it. Law also frustrates grace because man's sinful nature is enticed by it; that which law denies becomes desirable:

The sting of death is sin; and the strength of sin is the law. (1 Cor 15:56)

The practice of law-works is the opposite of accepting God's grace by faith. They are wholly incompatible:

And if by grace, then is it no more of works: otherwise grace is no more grace. But if it be of works, then is it no more grace: otherwise work is no more work. (Ro 11:6)

Where is boasting then? It is excluded. By what law? of works? Nay: but by the law (principle) of faith. Therefore we conclude that a man is justified by faith without the deeds of the law. (Ro 3:27-28, clarification added)

For if Abraham were justified by works, he hath whereof to glory; but not before God. For what saith the scripture? Abraham believed God, and it was counted unto him for righteousness. Now to him that worketh is the reward not reckoned of grace, but of debt. But to him that worketh not, but believeth on him that justifieth the ungodly, his faith is counted for righteousness. Even as David also describeth the blessedness of the man, unto whom God imputeth righteousness without works, Saying, Blessed are they whose iniquities are forgiven, and whose sins are covered. Blessed is the man to whom the Lord will not impute sin. (Ro 4:2-8)

> Law and grace are wholly incompatible.

Knowing that a man is not justified by the works of the law, but by the faith of Jesus Christ, even we have believed in Jesus Christ, that we might be justified by the faith of Christ, and not by the works of the law: for by the works of the law shall no flesh be justified. (Gal 2:16)

The justification of the believer before God is by faith in Jesus Christ, not by works. The testimony of scripture is also clear that the administration of the church is by grace, not by the Mosaic Law:

For sin shall not have dominion over you: for ye are not under the law, but under grace. (Ro 6:14)

But if ye be led of the Spirit, ye are not under the law. (Gal 5:18)

Be not thou therefore ashamed of the testimony of our Lord, nor of me his prisoner: but be thou partaker of the afflictions *of the gospel according to the power of God; Who hath saved us, and called us with an holy calling, **not according to our works**, but according to his own purpose and grace, which was given us in Christ Jesus before the world began, But is now made manifest by the appearing of our Saviour Jesus Christ, who hath abolished death, and hath brought life and immortality to light through the gospel...* (2 Tim 1:8-10)

Adding to the hopelessness of law-keeping is that Old Testament legalists cannot honestly claim to keep the Law, which included temple sacrifices and stonings, for example. They can only select parts of Israel's law to follow. But the Law is one entity, a complete and indivisible package, representing God's holiness.

> For Christ is the end of the law ... (Ro 10:4a)

Breaking any part of it breaks His entire Law, and performing only part of it does not qualify as keeping the Law. Trying to keep some fragment of the Law is a futile religious exercise.

For whosoever shall keep the whole law, and yet offend in one point, he is guilty of all. (Jas 2:10)

*For as many as are of the works of the law are under the curse: for it is written Cursed is every one that continueth not in all things which are written in the book of the law to do them. But that **no man is justified by the law** in the sight of God, it is evident: for, The just shall live by faith. And the law is not of faith: but, The man that doeth them shall live in them. Christ hath redeemed us from the curse of the law, being made a curse for us: for it is written, Cursed is every one that hangeth on a tree...* (Gal 3:10-13)

For I testify again to every man that is circumcised, that he is a debtor to do the whole law. Christ is become of no effect unto you, whosoever of you are justified by the law; ye are fallen from grace. (Gal 5:3-4)

For Christ is the end of the law for righteousness to every one that believeth. For Moses describeth the righteousness which is of the law, That the man which doeth those things shall live by them. (Ro 10:4-5)

Christians are not throwing out the Old Testament by not keeping the Law. We recognize that the Law had its role, as did the Garden of Eden, Noah's ark, Solomon's temple, and many other things that are not part of God's current program. We see the Law for what it was and walk by grace through faith, a vastly superior program given to administer the body of Christ (Heb 7:19, 7:22, 8:6).

OBJECTION 10

"I do my best and try to be a good person. I've lived a pretty good life, never cheated on my wife, or used drugs, or killed anyone. I sure don't live like so-and-so. I don't think I'm that bad that I deserve to burn in hell!"

Some who object to what Jesus did seem to have little awareness of their sinfulness. Such a person knows of people "worse" than he is, and therefore, the death, burial, and resurrection of Jesus Christ for sins is irrelevant. He has a law of his own which goes something like this: "Whatever I do is good enough by my own standard." God's evaluation of his life might be helpful to this objector.

It is God's standard, not ours, that will determine our eternal destiny, and judgment day is coming. The scripture is clear, both about mankind's lack of righteousness, and about the destination of those who refuse the righteousness offered by Christ. From the viewpoint of the Law, no one is good.

> There is none righteous, no, not one ... (Ro 3:10b)

Because so many people believe that they are good, we encourage you to do additional preparation for this objection by studying Chapter 3 of Romans. (See also Ps 14:1-3, 53:1-3)

And I saw the dead, small and great, stand before God; and the books were opened: and another book was opened, which is the book of life: and the dead were judged out of those things which were written in the books, according to their works. And the sea gave up the dead which were in it; and death and hell delivered up the dead which were in them: and they were judged every man according to their works. And death and hell were cast into the lake of fire. This is the second death. And whosoever was not found written in the book of life was cast into the lake of fire. (Rev 20:12-15)

God hates sin, and heaven would not be heavenly with sinners in it, so every sin must be sent away. Only with the righteousness of Jesus Christ can we enter into the presence of the Father (Jn 16:8-11). A person who believes in his own goodness, or who thinks he only needs to be better than somebody else, might not be open to the Gospel until he recognizes his own sinfulness before God. Sometimes asking him questions about his foibles and failings can trigger some awareness. Whether or not he believes the testimony of scripture regarding his condition could depend upon his level of respect for the Bible. This objector must accept that only by faith in Jesus' death, burial, and resurrection for sin can one attain His righteousness and enter heaven.

OBJECTION 11

"I've been a Christian my whole life. I was born in a Christian home, I was baptized and confirmed, I go to church, pray, and have even read the whole Bible. I am offended that you would bring up salvation!"

An objection which comes from a church attendee is sometimes the most difficult to overcome. Such an objector might be proclaiming grace, but in practice he is legalistic, adding works to the Gospel. Legalism can be strict, structured law-keeping, but it can also be soft, personalized "do-good-ism," which not only seems harmless, but is altruistic, even sacrificial. This person does not see that he follows a law of his own making, a set of standards by which he measures his

> For Christ sent me not to baptize, but to preach the gospel ... (1 Cor 1:17a)

"Christianity." Such a system is likely to include religious acts such as water baptism, confirmation, or attendance at church classes and groups which increase his confidence in his position before God. His religious life may be some version of "comparing themselves among themselves," considering himself a Christian because his lifestyle choices are superior to the choices of others (2 Cor 10:12). He could also view Christianity to be something one is born into, like being born into an Irish family. For him, the death, burial, and resurrection of Christ is almost a non-issue because Christianity is his lifestyle. He is "living the Christian life," …except without the life part.

"Lifestyle Christianity" aka The Good People

Because of the prevalence of the view of Christianity as a lifestyle, it deserves further attention. Many people define Christianity in the same way as does the world at large; it comes through cultural affiliation, the receiving of sacraments, or some other external means. Viewing the Christian faith as a moral lifestyle choice is an indirect objection to what Jesus did, because His work is not the object of faith. This objector may be aware that he does not even meet his own standard of morality, but he is doing a better job than the next guy, whose standard is lower. His reasoning does not take into account that the standard for heaven is God's perfect holiness, which cannot be achieved by lifestyle choices, however upstanding they might be.

Christianity is a spiritual birth, not a lifestyle. It is not passed on through a family. It is not conferred through baptism or any other church activity. Without spiritual regeneration, we are merely trying to live our best in our sinful flesh, and we cannot enter into a relationship with God. When sharing the Gospel with

> Christianity is a spiritual birth, not a lifestyle.

a hearer who is stuck on the idea that he is living a Christian lifestyle, you will need to distinguish external moral living from the new birth, which is explained in Chapter One. It is spiritual regeneration, not good living, that makes us Christians. We are born again by faith in the message of 1 Corinthians 15:1-4, the Gospel of Christ, and by no other means.

OBJECTION 12

"What about all the good things I have done? I think I have done more good than evil. In the end, I think my good deeds will outweigh my bad deeds."

This objection represents the essential philosophy of perhaps every non-biblical faith that has ever existed. If salvation is not a free gift from God, then it is up to the individual to do what he can to earn eternity. The Bible stands alone in denying the possibility of works for salvation.

> *Not by works of righteousness which we have done, but according to his mercy he saved us, by the washing of regeneration, and renewing of the Holy Ghost ...* (Titus 3:5)

Balancing Act

This classic version of works for salvation is represented by the good old scale of balance which compares my good works to my bad works, instead of comparing all my works to the work of Jesus Christ crucified. Characterizing God's judgment as a scale or balance, like

> It is Christ's sacrifice alone which provides salvation.

a statue of Lady Justice in a courtroom, has an inherent problem, however. Lady Justice is not comparing good deeds to bad deeds; she is weighing evidence! Is there evidence that I am a sinner? Yes, indeed; we all are. As with every legalistic thinker, the objector who weighs good against bad has set his own standard, and has determined his case in his own favor. He believes that he has done more good than harm.

The Bible contains nothing to support the idea that one can do a certain number of "bad deeds" as long as a greater amount of good is done. If it did, how would "bad" be measured? What qualifies as bad? How much "good" needs to be done for each bad deed? Since the Bible's judgment has already been excluded, whose estimation of good is used? The problem with this view quickly becomes apparent upon scrutiny.

Far from accepting a certain amount of sin, God, the perfect judge, is holy and is offended by all sin. Only a corrupt judge would exonerate a man for murder because he once saved someone's life. To think that Almighty God would implement such a system is not reasonable, because a system that balances good deeds against bad is allowing those bad deeds and deeming them permissible, as long as they are "balanced with good."

In reality, how many "good deeds" does a person ever really do? Most things that people do are out of necessity and self-interest. Meeting obligations, obeying laws, and fulfilling agreements can hardly be characterized as "good deeds." Some religions count every prayer as a good deed, but for what do most people pray? Are most of the world's prayers for wants and wishes? How many plead as David did to do nothing but the will of God (Ps 143:10)? The person who is relying upon an accumulation of good deeds is also trusting in his own evaluation of them. He is not trusting in the death, burial, and resurrection of Jesus Christ for his salvation. Each person must be convinced that the Gospel of Christ, found in 1 Corinthians 15:1-4, is true and, therefore, sufficient to save him.

OBJECTION 13

"I don't agree with you; I have my own beliefs."
"I sincerely believe in my faith, and I think God will honor that."
"God and I have an understanding."

Yet another way to object to the value of what Jesus did is to deny the unique nature of His ministry to humanity. This objector counts any religious belief valid, and, therefore, whatever form that belief takes becomes a personal works system. He assumes that God will bow to whatever religion he wishes to practice. Putting himself in God's place,

> Sanctify them through thy truth: thy word is truth. (Jn 17:17)

he makes God submissive to his idea or plan. In this view, the sacrifice of Jesus for sin is of no greater value than any fanciful religious notion.

> *There is a way which seemeth right unto a man, but the end thereof are the ways of death.* (Prov 14:12)

Wishful Thinking

For the person who has his own unique beliefs about Christianity, or feels comfortable in the religion of his choice, "sincerity" is often used as the standard and the measure of faith. It is truth, however, and not sincerity that matters to God. What evidence does the objector have that what he believes is true? Is there evidence that God honors false religion if it is practiced with sincerity? The Bible claims to be *the truth*; therefore, its author cannot approve of competing and contradictory faith claims. If the hearer has little respect for or belief in the Bible, he may refuse to consider scripture references. But as ministers of the Gospel, we can attempt to offer information and answer questions, allowing the Spirit of God to do His convincing work as to the truth of scripture:

> *Jesus saith unto him, I am the way, the truth, and the life: no man cometh unto the Father, but by me.* (Jn 14:6)

> *And this is life eternal, that they might know thee the only true God, and Jesus Christ, whom thou hast sent.* (Jn 17:3)

> *And for their sakes I sanctify myself, that they also might be sanctified through the truth.* (Jn 17:19)

> *In whom ye also trusted, after that ye heard the word of truth, the gospel of your salvation: in whom also after that ye believed, ye were sealed with that holy Spirit of promise.* (Eph 1:13)

> *For the hope which is laid up for you in heaven, whereof ye heard before in the word of the truth of the gospel.* (Col 1:5)

> *For this cause also thank we God without ceasing, because, when ye received the word of God which ye heard of us, ye received it not as the word of men, but as it is in truth, the*

word of God, which effectually worketh also in you that
believe. (1 Thes 2:13)

But we are bound to give thanks alway to God for you,
brethren beloved of the Lord, because God hath from the
beginning chosen you to salvation through sanctification of the
Spirit and belief of the truth... (2 Thes 2:13)

Who will have all men to be saved, and to come unto the
knowledge of the truth. (1 Tim 2:4)

But if I tarry long, that thou mayest know how thou oughtest
to behave thyself in the house of God, which is the church of
the living God, the pillar and ground of the truth. (1 Tim 3:15)

To see the truth means to see things as they really are. Only God
can see the truth of all things, therefore we need His word to teach
us what is true. A person can be sincere and yet be wrong. Therefore,
regardless of one's sincerity in believing
a lie, in regard to eternity, only that
which is true is of value. The world is
full of facts, but the Bible, God's word
to mankind, is truth.

> ... the truth shall
> make you free.
> (Jn 8:32b)

Many hearers of the Gospel of Christ will object to what Jesus did.
They might insist that more must be done, denying that faith in
Christ's finished work is sufficient to save. Others will define
Christianity as merely moral living, disregarding what Jesus did
altogether. To meet some moral lifestyle standard, an adherent to
this belief will need to follow a "do and don't" system, rather than
accepting Jesus' payment for sins on the cross by faith. Including
some behaviors and excluding others for the purpose of salvation
is a form of legalism, an external system of rules. Christianity

specifically excludes itself as a law system, proclaiming that God's law had a purpose which has since been fulfilled (Gal 3:24-25).

Christianity is a spiritual birth: an internal change by grace through faith. A godly lifestyle is the outworking of that internal change, not its cause (Phil 2:12). The issue of legalism is vast and complex. As with every objection

> Not by works of righteousness which we have done, but according to his mercy he saved us ... (Titus 3:5a)

to the Gospel, a Christian's best tool is a thorough understanding of the Gospel by which we are saved, found in 1 Corinthians 15:1-4.

_____

_____

_____

F O U R

WHY I NEED IT

For Sin

Objections to the Gospel of Christ take many forms and are commonly about specific doctrines such as the deity of Christ, the sufficiency of grace, or the authority of the Bible. When a person is asked a question about his faith, he could raise another type of objection which might be more challenging to a Christian witness because it is not about a particular teaching. Rather than taking issue with the particulars of Christianity, some hearers are disinterested, lacking concern about eternity and salvation. They might find matters of faith to be foolish or a waste of time. Some believe they are already "good with God," while others are not concerned because they do not believe in the afterlife. They are in denial regarding their sinful state and their accountability to their Creator. Wanting to follow their own way, they reject their need for a solution to sin.

OBJECTION 14

"What is someone dying on a cross going to do for me? Religion is for other people, and a crutch for the weak. I don't need saving."

To better understand why salvation is needed, it helps to compare the problem of sin to earthly justice. Going to jail or prison used to be referred to as "paying a debt to society." The phrase recognizes that when someone commits a crime, he has harmed his community or a member of it. Since the criminal cannot undo what has been done, he must pay for his crime in some way, such as with a fine, imprisonment, or even with his life. Committing a sin also creates a debt, but with God:

> "*Against thee, thee only, have I sinned...*" (Ps 51:4a).

Even a person who does not acknowledge wronging God is unlikely to claim that he has never done anything wrong. Each of us has a God-given conscience, and we all know—or at least hope—that our lives and actions matter. Therefore, the real reason for objecting to the Gospel might not be due to disbelieving in sin, but in not wanting to be held accountable for it. Man is a sinner by nature, and sin's

> It is a fearful thing to fall into the hands of the living God. (Heb 10:31)

hallmark is rebellion against God. God's assessment of mankind can be helpful in breaking down a hearer's denial of the need for a solution to sin. The Bible tells us that we are born in sin, and that there is a consequence for sin:

> *Behold, I was shapen in iniquity; and in sin did my mother conceive me.* (Ps 51:5)

But we are all as an unclean thing, and all our righteousnesses are as filthy rags; and we all do fade as a leaf; and our iniquities, like the wind, have taken us away. (Isa 64:6)

And Jesus said unto him, Why callest thou me good? there is none good but one, that is, God. (Mk 10:18; see also Mt 19:17; Lk 18:19)

For the wages of sin is death; but the gift of God is eternal life through Jesus Christ our Lord. (Ro 6:23)

Therefore thou art inexcusable, O man, whosoever thou art that judgest: for wherein thou judgest another, thou condemnest thyself; for thou that judgest doest the same things. But we are sure that the judgment of God is according to truth against them which commit such things. And thinkest thou this, O man, that judgest them which do such things, and doest the same, that thou shalt escape the judgment of God? Or despisest thou the riches of his goodness and forbearance and longsuffering; not knowing that the goodness of God leadeth thee to repentance? But after thy hardness and impenitent heart treasurest up unto thyself wrath against the day of wrath and revelation of the righteous judgment of God; Who will render to every man according to his deeds … In the day when God shall judge the secrets of men by Jesus Christ according to my gospel. (Ro 2:1-6, 16)

> … none is good, save one, that is, God. (Lk 18:19)

Each of us is tainted by sin in all we desire, think, say, and do. God's conclusion regarding mankind's goodness is, "There is none that does good, there is not even one" (Ro 3:12b NASB). Any person who is not as good as God is not qualified for heaven, and nothing he produces is good enough either. Remaining in denial about one's accountability to his Creator is a stall but not a solution. One day every person will face God and be held to account for what he did and said:

> *Nothing in all creation is hidden from God's sight. Everything is uncovered and laid bare before the eyes of him to whom we must give account.* (Heb 4:13 NIV)

Each person must decide for himself whether he believes the Gospel of Christ, the message which declares God's solution to the problem of sin. The hearer may insist that "religion" is not for him, but if he acknowledges that he has offended God, perhaps he will

> ... every one of us shall give account of himself to God. (Ro 14:12)

consider the Bible's warning that he needs Jesus Christ to pay for his sins. If not, he will be separated from God forever, paying for his own sins in the lake of fire:

> *And the devil that deceived them was cast into the lake of fire and brimstone, where the beast and the false prophet are, and shall be tormented day and night for ever and ever. And I saw a great white throne, and him that sat on it, from whose face the earth and the heaven fled away; and there was found no place for them. And I saw the dead, small and great, stand before God; and the books were opened: and another book was opened, which is the book of life: and the dead were judged out of those things which were written in the books, according to their works. And the sea gave up the dead which were in it; and death and hell delivered up the dead which were in them: and they were judged every man according to their works.*

And death and hell were cast into the lake of fire. This is the
second death. And whosoever was not found written in the
book of life was cast into the lake of fire. (Rev 20:10-15)

Avoiding the lake of fire seems like a good reason to consider
salvation. Jesus gave Himself as the object of God's wrath against
sin, taking our punishment and dying in our place. Upon believing
the Gospel, the sinner is credited with the payment for sin made
by Jesus Christ on his behalf. Jesus' payment satisfied both the
justice and the love of God; the sin debt is justly satisfied, and the
sinner is lovingly released from the debt.

What About the Cross?

Part of the objection to one's need for salvation may be a lack of
appreciation for what was accomplished on the cross. From the
perspective of such objectors, many people died on a cross, so
Jesus' death is not special. This unique death, however, fulfilled
many biblical prophecies (Ps 22:1-18, 31:5, 34:20, 69:21; Is 50:6,
52:14, 53:1-12; Zech 11:12-13, 12:10).

It is God who chose this method for the Savior's death. The Bible
does not explain why a cross was used, but perhaps the horrific
nature of this manner of death was intended to portray the
seriousness of sin. The Bible states that dying on a tree displayed
that the person was cursed by God:

Christ hath redeemed us from the curse of the law, being
made a curse for us: for it is written, Cursed is every one that
hangeth on a tree... (Gal 3:13)

And if a man have committed a sin worthy of death, and he
be to be put to death, and thou hang him on a tree: His body

shall not remain all night upon the tree, but thou shalt in any wise bury him that day; (for he that is hanged is accursed of God;) that thy land be not defiled, which the LORD thy God giveth thee for an inheritance. (Deut 21:22-23)

Sin is a curse upon mankind, and the death of our Savior provided release from that curse for all who believe the Gospel of Christ. A person who denies any accountability for sin, or insists that faith is for the weak, could be using the objections as a defense or holding them as sincere beliefs. In any case, our calling as Christians is to proclaim that faith in Jesus' sacrifice provides the deliverance from sin that every person needs.

He has fixed a day in which He will judge the world in righteousness through a Man whom He has appointed, having furnished proof to all men by raising Him from the dead. (Acts 17:31 NASB)

OBJECTION 15

"My lifestyle is not a sin; God made me this way. Why should I believe a religion that says that I am not okay the way I am?"

As a culture, our interest in religion increasingly comes more from a consumer's viewpoint than from a sinner's. "What will it do for me?" is the mantra of our day, and behaviors formerly considered sin have been embraced. One would think that the consumer mindset would welcome the vast benefits of salvation, but it is not so, because society has rejected the view of mankind as sinners. Couple this attitude with the issues of sexuality and gender which have been pushed to the forefront of social discussion, and we find people standing in judgment of God for His disagreement with their views. This breath-taking stance is often defended with claims that some sins are traits which existed from birth, an issue which matters no more than whether a person was born with any other preference. A person's preferences have no bearing whatsoever on the fact that God both expects and deserves to be believed and obeyed.

> ... be ye reconciled to God. (2 Cor 5:20b)

The real issue is not when our preferences develop, but that there is a difference between what we do and who we are. Regardless of *which* sins we do or don't practice, who we are is described in one word: sinners. Each man's nature leads him to seek or deny his preferences, indulging or suppressing them to varying degrees, depending upon his willpower and convictions. Regardless of one's views of how we each developed our own particular brand of sin, God still asks us to live according to His will, and does not give special exception to any group of people or category of behavior. Our own nature, preferences, will, or desires provide no excuse before God. If we deny our need for salvation from sin, He allows us to follow sin to its ultimate consequence:

> *Because that which may be known of God is manifest in them;*
> *for God hath shewed it unto them. For the invisible things*
> *of him from the creation of the world are clearly seen, being*
> *understood by the things that are made, even his eternal power*

and Godhead; so that they are without excuse: Because that,
when they knew God, they glorified him not as God, neither
were thankful; but became vain in their imaginations, and
their foolish heart was darkened. … And even as they did not
like to retain God in their knowledge, God gave them over to a
reprobate mind, to do those things which are not convenient;
Being filled with all unrighteousness, fornication, wickedness,
covetousness, maliciousness; full of envy, murder, debate,
deceit, malignity; whisperers, Backbiters, haters of God,
despiteful, proud, boasters, inventors of evil things, disobedient
to parents, Without understanding, covenantbreakers, without
natural affection, implacable, unmerciful: Who knowing the
judgment of God, that they which commit such things are
worthy of death, not only do the same, but have pleasure in
them that do them. (Ro 1:19-21, 28-32)

A hearer may have many reasons for denying his need for salvation, but the bottom line is that he does not want it. Rejecting the Gospel is an avoidance of the real issue, which is sin. Christian witnesses need not be drawn into debates about the nature of sinful tendencies. We are to share the Gospel, and if the hearer believes, he will learn that God does not approve of every whim and desire of mankind. The believer who yields to the power of grace can also experience freedom from the power of sin. A holy God has standards. A powerful God provides deliverance. A loving God proclaims that the needed solution to sin is free, and can be found in 1 Corinthians 15:1-4.

OBJECTION 16

"I make mistakes, but I wouldn't call myself a sinner."

This objection to the need for salvation begs the question, "What does this person think a sinner is?" A correct definition of sin might be all that is needed to answer this objection. Jesus died for the sins of the world because every human being is a sinner, having fallen short of the glory of God. We don't have to do much to fall short of glory! God is perfect, and is offended by sin; we are indebted to God for disobeying Him. Jesus paid the sin debt that we owe by taking the punishment for sin upon Himself on the cross.

A common misunderstanding of sin is that being a sinner means that a person is "really bad" or does horrifically evil deeds. Some divide wrongs into seemingly harmless categories such as "little white lies," but God does not. In Revelation we see that liars are headed for the lake of fire right along with murderers. The point is that for God, sin is sin. All sin separates us from Him because God is holy.

> *But the fearful, and unbelieving, and the abominable, and murderers, and whoremongers, and sorcerers, and idolaters, and all liars, shall have their part in the lake which burneth with fire and brimstone: which is the second death. (Rev 21:8)*

> *These six things doth the LORD hate: yea, seven are an abomination unto him: A proud look, a lying tongue, and hands that shed innocent blood, An heart that deviseth wicked imaginations, feet that be swift in running to mischief, A false witness that speaketh lies, and he that soweth discord among brethren. (Prov 6:16-19)*

Adam and Eve in the garden of Eden are good examples of this principle. Adam's sin was the worst sin in the history of mankind, bringing humanity from perfection to a cursed world, from innocence to a knowledge of evil, and from bliss to pain. Eating a piece of off-limits fruit would not typically be considered a horrific act; it was acting independently from God which made it so. God cursed the entire earth for one sin, so comparing God's evaluation of sin to his own may lead this objector to reconsider his standard for what makes someone a sinner. Sin doesn't just mean evil; it can be anything that is not according to God's will. Helping hearers understand how God defines sin is part of helping them to see why they need salvation. We are either perfect or we are sinners, and sinners need a savior.

> ... for whatsoever is not of faith is sin. (Ro 14:23b)

For all have sinned and come short of the glory of God. (Ro 3:23)

OBJECTION 17

"I'll worry about getting saved later, sometime before I die."

Another way of objecting to one's need for what Jesus did is procrastination. It is a flawed plan, since no person knows how much time he has on earth. A Christian witness can suggest to the one objecting that he might not have an opportunity to make a lucid decision on his deathbed, and encourage him to consider the Gospel now. Even if the hearer is not open to believing the Gospel of Christ, if he listens to the details of 1 Corinthians 15:1-4 now, he will

> ... now is the accepted time ... now is the day of salvation. (2 Cor 6:2b)

have more information when his final day comes.

> *Yet you do not know what your life will be like tomorrow. You are just a vapor that appears for a little while and then vanishes away.* (Jas 4:14 NASB)

> *Like as a father pitieth his children, so the LORD pitieth them that fear him. For he knoweth our frame; he remembereth that we are dust. As for man, his days are as grass: as a flower of the field, so he flourisheth. For the wind passeth over it, and it is gone; and the place thereof shall know it no more.* (Ps 103:13-16)

OBJECTION 18

"I'm already a Christian. I just don't believe _____."

Sometimes an objector does not know he is an objector because he sees no incompatibility between being a Christian and rejecting some of Christianity's tenets. Excusing oneself from a particular doctrine could come from an unbeliever who needs to hear the

Gospel, or from a believer who does not understand the significance of scriptural authority. Perhaps, for example, the objector claims to be a Christian, but denies hell. A Christian witness should explain to him that hell is a penalty for sin, and that if there is no penalty, there is no need for a savior. Without the Savior, there is no Christianity, because

> ... thy word is truth. (Jn 17:17b)

the object of our faith is our Savior and what He did for us. Following his objection to its logical conclusion will expose the problem of excluding this doctrine from Christian belief. If he is a Christian, recognizing the incompatibility of his belief with the Gospel will sometimes result in an immediate change of mind.

If explaining the objectionable doctrine does not bring about an "aha moment," the question becomes why this person does not believe the testimony of the Bible on the doctrine he objects to. Of immediate importance to a Christian witness is whether the disputed doctrine is a component of the Gospel of Christ. If it is, or if you are not sure how much of the Gospel the objector believes, attempt to engage him in a discussion of 1 Corinthians 15:1-4. Gather as much information as you can about his understanding of it. While additional objections may arise during the conversation and can be addressed, of primary importance is that you provide as much information as he is willing to hear about the way of salvation.

_____

_____

_____

OBJECTION 19

"I don't need Jesus. There is nothing after death, just lights out."

Sometimes denying one's need of salvation is coupled with the atheistic view that man is only a material being and that there is nothing beyond this world. Such a view denies the source of all morality, and yet the person who holds it almost certainly raises his children with rules, feels badly when he hurts someone, and likes to see justice done when a wrong is committed. The existence of man's conscience informs us that we are more than material beings. Material cannot create the concepts of right and wrong, nor any other spiritual concept, such as liberty, beauty, or happiness. Exposing the contradiction between denying the existence of spiritual life while living by its principles may cause this person to consider that there is more to human existence than what we see.

> *For when the Gentiles, which have not the law, do by nature*
> *the things contained in the law, these, having not the law,*
> *are a law unto themselves: Which shew the work of the law*
> *written in their hearts, their conscience also bearing witness,*
> *and their thoughts the mean while accusing or else excusing*
> *one another ...* (Ro 2:14-15)

Another problem with the notion of man as material only is that it makes life completely pointless. For example, if death is just "lights out," why should any person bother acting rightly? If there is no judgment at the end, maybe we should stop trying so hard for a "better world" and relax a little. Doing more of what we want might be a better option than trying to follow all the world's rules. We can do good all our lives, but in a generation or two most of us will be forgotten anyway. In this world, most of our lives don't amount to much, and then we don't exist anymore.

But most people do not believe that we no longer exist after death, or that our lives and actions do not matter. We believe that how we raise our children, our faithfulness in marriage, and our honesty at work all have greater meaning than just the earthly rewards for doing so. Perhaps this objector will follow up by saying that doing rightly makes the world more enjoyable while we are here. While this is so, it does not explain how it is that people everywhere share so much agreement on what

> The fool hath said in his heart, There is no God. (Ps 14:1a)

constitutes good and bad. Perhaps that is so because these ideas have a common source. The Bible informs us that we all have a God-given conscience. It also says that faith is reasonable and disbelief is foolish, and that judgment day is coming. Not only does our conscience proclaim the existence of God, the creation displays it too. God's word has also been proven true by the resurrection of Jesus Christ:

> He has fixed a day in which He will judge the world in righteousness through a Man whom He has appointed, having furnished proof to all men by raising Him from the dead. (Acts 17:31 NASB)

> And that we may be delivered from unreasonable and wicked men: for all men have not faith. (2 Thes 3:2)

> For what if some did not believe? Will their unbelief make the faithfulness of God without effect? Certainly not! Indeed, let God be true but every man a liar. (Ro 3:3-4a NKJV)

Because that which may be known of God is manifest in them; for God hath shewed it unto them. For the invisible things of him from the creation of the world are clearly seen, being understood by the things that are made, even his eternal power and Godhead; so that they are without excuse. (Ro 1:19-20)

What we do, what we think, and even our motives matter. Eternity matters and it is real. Our Christian calling is to testify to the truth of scripture to all who will listen, helping them to see why they need salvation. It is left to the conscience and will of each hearer to believe the Gospel of Christ… or not to.

OBJECTION 20

"I don't need religion; I am close to God when I ___." "I'm a very spiritual person."

Another objection to why we need the Gospel is a belief held by many, that they have their "own way" to be close to God. God, however, has already revealed the way in which we can be close to Him, and He will not defer to whatever way a person conceives. We are all sinners who need salvation, and it is only possible through His Son, the Lord Jesus Christ, by faith in the Gospel message of 1 Corinthians 15:1-4.

Although many claim to have found their own way to God, God's actual way is not difficult to find. As is commonly known by Christians, but may not be known by the hearer, the death, burial, and resurrection of Jesus Christ for sin is a well-documented event in ancient history, and the Bible has been the best-selling book for as long as there have been books to sell. Amazingly, although many Christians suffer, are persecuted, and have every reason to abandon Jesus, the world sees that the faith has not been extinguished. Suggest to a hearer that God's way may be worth hearing about and considering. He might

> There is a way which seemeth right unto a man, but the end thereof are the ways of death. (Prov 14:12)

agree that there is some value in looking at facts, rather than assuming that an idea he has in his own mind is acceptable to God.

A witnessing opportunity may or may not be the time to address the definition of spirituality, but it is not what most people probably think it is. To be spiritual means to emanate the character of God by way of the filling of God Himself. His virtues are produced in the believer by the Holy Spirit, and are known as the fruit of the Spirit (Gal 5:22-23). Being spiritual is only possible for those who have been born again.

If the hearer agrees that there is a God, he might also agree that He has His own ideas about how things should be done. The Bible is a credible authority to learn about God and why we need Him. We can suggest to hearers that it might be worth learning about rather than dismissed, and help them see why they need God's one and only way of salvation.

_____

_____

_____

OBJECTION 21

"Christians are hypocrites. Why should I be held accountable for what I do, when that famous Christian did _____?!"

It is not uncommon for people to judge Christianity by the disobedience of a few. Christian witnesses who face this objection to why we need the Gospel can share several points with hearers who focus on the sins or hypocrisy of somebody else. Firstly, Christians are individuals, so claiming that all are hypocrites, for example, is simply not factual. Secondly, what some people do in disobedience to the faith is not the fault of God or the faith, and therefore not a reason to reject it. Thirdly, every person will one day face God with his sins, regardless of whether it appears as if he got away with something in the present time. Denying one's need of a remedy for sin does not remove anyone from God's final accounting for sin. When compared to the non-believing world, God's people are held to a much higher standard in our earthly lives:

> For whom the Lord loveth he chasteneth, and scourgeth every son whom he receiveth. If ye endure chastening, God dealeth with you as with sons; for what son is he whom the father chasteneth not? (Heb 12:6-7)

> What then? are we better than they? No, in no wise: for we have before proved both Jews and Gentiles, that they are all under sin; As it is written, There is none righteous, no, not one ... (Ro 3:9-10)

The Bible is not a leaflet for a reason; everybody needs much instruction and has much to learn. There is not a person alive who lives in perfect accordance with his own values, much less God's, so anyone can be deemed a hypocrite. Encourage a hearer to look to his own failings, then offer him the solution: faith in the Gospel of Christ. Share with him that Christians are forgiven, but they have no license to sin. Some even face discipline from their Father for persistent sin, but on judgment day, they will not pay with their lives. Jesus already paid with His.

> *Come now, and let us reason together, saith the LORD: though your sins be as scarlet, they shall be as white as snow; though they be red like crimson, they shall be as wool.* (Isa 1:18)

OBJECTION 22

"I can believe what I want."

Absolutely, yes you can! This objector might be assuming that you are going to argue the point or try to force your beliefs on him. You can instead delight him with the fact that you agree; he can indeed believe what he wants to. He might not, however, enjoy the result of entrusting his life to an idea which has no merit. The idea of having some evidence of his eternal destiny could appeal to this objector. He might also recognize that in any situation, there is a problem with believing things which are not true. Crossing one's fingers and hoping to be right is not the wisest course to take in life, let alone in eternity. Share with him that the same God who allows him to do and believe what he likes is also his Creator, who loved him in the sacrifice of Christ, and has readied a wonderful future for him; he need only believe.

For the time is come that judgment must begin at the house of God: and if it first begin at us, what shall the end be of them that obey not the gospel of God? And if the righteous scarcely be saved, where shall the ungodly and the sinner appear?
(1 Pet 4:17-18)

_____

_____

_____

F I V E

HOW TO GET IT

Believe

T
o gain salvation from sin and its consequences, one must believe the Gospel of Christ. Leading others to this conclusion is the goal of asking them a question about the Bible, the Gospel, Jesus, or their own ideas regarding faith. Perhaps the most common objection to faith—the "how" of salvation—is that simply believing is not sufficient, a topic covered in Chapter Three. Simple faith is a concept that many find difficult to accept. Some deny the need to exercise faith. Others replace faith with religious activities or equate faith in the Gospel of Christ with the faith claims of other religions. Some dismiss faith, claiming that truth cannot be known, while others define faith incorrectly, considering it an unproven "leap in the dark." But contrary to the idea of a "blind leap" of faith, God provided a large book of evidence for the Christian faith to rest upon. Whether by denying the simplicity, exclusivity, or necessity of it, those who deny that believing the Gospel is the way to access salvation do have faith in something, even if it is only in their own surmising. Reasoned

explanations to their objections can help hearers to place their faith correctly—in Jesus Christ and His payment for the sins of the world.

> For the message of the cross is foolishness to those who are perishing, but to us who are being saved it is the power of God. (1 Cor 1:18, NKJV)

OBJECTION 23

"Jesus died for the sins of the world, so everyone is saved. They may not know Jesus, but He still died for their sins."
"All roads lead to heaven."

Salvation is not unconditional; there is a singular condition: faith. The object of Christian faith is described in the saving message found in 1 Corinthians 15:1-4. This passage explains that it is the death, burial, and resurrection of Jesus Christ for sins, according to the scriptures, that saves each one who believes.

Denying that faith is the condition for salvation can take a "Christian" or non-Christian form. Some "believe in Jesus" in such a way as to conclude that everyone has already been saved because of Him. The non-Christian version of this is the idea of universal salvation regardless of one's brand of religion. Christianity is accused of narrow-mindedness for requiring a condition, or for claiming the one and only way of salvation, but it is the idea of universal salvation which is narrow, offering only one destiny to all, while God offers two. The Gospel provides a choice: to go to heaven or hell, to live in communion or in separateness, to believe or reject the will of our Creator.

Denying the requirement of faith is a larger objection than simply denying the existence of a condition for salvation. It denies the word of God which declares it, the Christian's calling to proclaim it, and the choice of man to refuse or accept it. This objector may think himself generous and compassionate for releasing others from the requirement to believe the Gospel, but he is actually making himself a barrier to salvation. Denying that a condition exists may seem to him to eliminate the threat of hell, but offering false hope does the opposite

> Therefore it is of faith, that it might be by grace...
> (Romans 4:16a)

of what he intends. To be saved from the penalty of sin, each person must believe the Gospel of Christ, found in 1 Corinthians 15:1-4.

> *He that believeth on him is not condemned: but he that believeth not is condemned already, because he hath not believed in the name of the only begotten Son of God.* (Jn 3:18)

OBJECTION 24

"What about the people who haven't heard?" (aka "What about the guy in Bongo Bongo?")

The objection that we affectionately call "the guy in Bongo Bongo" is based on an imaginary man who has never heard the Gospel. The assumption made is that there are people who have no awareness of Christianity, which therefore implies the need for an alternate way to be saved. How we are saved is by hearing the Gospel, but since this is supposedly not available, God must accept whatever religious effort is made by "the guy in Bongo Bongo."

Despite the fact that man does as he wishes in rebellion against God, he remains persistently religious. When the human spirit is not used in accordance with its function to commune with God, man seeks another means of fulfillment, practicing religious rituals to elicit a response from his "god." Some conclude that the existence of false religion means that remote peoples are not able to find the truth,

> If any man will do his will, he shall know of the doctrine... (Jn 7:17a)

so whatever they happen to believe should be good enough for God.

Perhaps because of the influence of The Theory of Evolution, the perception exists that remote peoples are ignorant, involuntarily isolated, and have been doing very little for a very long time. Contrary to the notion that "primitive" peoples haven't "evolved," in actuality, remote societies have managed to survive, keeping themselves warm, fed, and sheltered. They have populated far-flung islands, made discoveries, and passed along survival skills for generations. They seem quite capable. Considering also that missionaries have been traveling and sharing information for two thousand years, we cannot assume that remote peoples have not heard.

From the Bible record we know that man has been man all along, with intelligence, skills, and abilities given by God. The "Bongo Bongo objection" is ultimately an attack on God's character, accusing Him of leaving people with no way to be saved. God, however, desires for all to be saved, because God is love. The existence of false religion does not mean that God has left some people with no way to find the truth, nor does it necessitate that God contradict His word and allow alternative ways of salvation. Bibles, churches, missionaries, and believers are everywhere. This objector can be assured that God will get the truth of how to be saved to those who want to know Him.

And ye shall seek me, and find me, when ye shall search for me with all your heart. (Jer 29:13)

Because that which may be known of God is manifest in them; for God hath shewed it unto them. For the invisible things of him from the creation of the world are clearly seen, being understood by the things that are made, even his eternal power and Godhead; so that they are without excuse ... (Ro 1:19-20)

For this is good and acceptable in the sight of God our Saviour; Who will have all men to be saved, and to come unto the knowledge of the truth. (1 Tim 2:3-4)

OBJECTION 25

"Faith in the Christian Gospel cannot be the only way to heaven. What about all the other religions?" "Different religions; same god."

Some objections to faith in the Gospel take issue with its exclusivity. With a custom-designed way of salvation for everyone, this "politically correct" view of religion is defeated by the fact that every religious belief cannot be true. Some are clearly invented to control and manipulate its followers. Some are preposterous. They deny and contradict each other, and have completely different gods, scriptures, and ways of salvation. This objector may not have considered the fact that most other

> ... no man cometh unto the Father, but by me. (Jn 14:6b)

religious systems have exclusive claims as well. Denying Christianity because of its exclusivity eliminates every religion with an exclusive claim, a fact which neutralizes this objection.

There is another problem with reasoning that there may be a way of salvation while denying that Christianity is that way. If Jesus is not the way of salvation, and a religion other than Christianity was "the one true faith," how would anyone know it? It would be an insurmountable problem to objectively evaluate all of the world's belief systems, evenly scoring each by its merits, historical accuracy, evidence, logic, and reasonableness in order to know what to believe. Many religions have been lost to history. What if one of those was "the one?" Thankfully we do not need to scour the earth to find the right one, nor settle for the conundrum of competing claims. The true God settled the question by revealing Himself to us. He stepped into time and changed the world forever. He provided a book that cannot be disproven and He changed the heart of man. Christianity is a "religion" like no other, not only because of the miraculous death, burial, and resurrection of Jesus, but also because it stands alone in declaring that man cannot save himself. False religions cannot guarantee anything; they cannot prove anything, and they cannot save. Our God, just as a loving father would, took it upon Himself to save us.

> *He saw that there was no man, And wondered that there was no intercessor; Therefore His own arm brought salvation for Him; And His own righteousness, it sustained Him.*
> (Isaiah 59:16 NKJV)

OBJECTION 26

"So you're saying no Hindus or Muslims or Buddhists are saved?"
"So you're saying my grandma is in hell?"
"So your belief is right and everybody else is wrong?!"

Sometimes an apparent objection to the Christian faith is due to the realization that the Gospel of Christ precludes another way of salvation. The objector could be reacting out of concern for loved ones who believed something other than the Gospel that is being presented to him. An objection of this sort can also be an attack on you as the messenger of the Gospel, as if you are a know-it-all, pronouncing the eternal destiny of others. The issue, however, is not about the beliefs of the Christian witness or anyone else; it is about what God has said in His word about how one is saved.

If someone has passed on, and what they believed is unknown, the hearer may take comfort in the character of the One who created us and died to save us. If the loved one wanted to know how to be saved, God would not have kept the truth hidden from him; He is drawing all men to Himself through the preaching of the Gospel.

> *No man can come to me, except the Father which hath*
> *sent me draw him: and I will raise him up at the last day.*
> (Jn 6:44)

Here in America especially, it is unlikely that someone would get through life without ever hearing the Gospel, attending church, or having access to a Bible. If an objector is accusing the witness of being a judge, this can be turned by pointing the hearer to scripture. The witness is not the authority,

> ... God is love
> (1 Jn 4:8b)

the Bible is. God's word explains salvation; the Christian witness is just a messenger.

When we share the message of salvation by faith alone, it can elicit strong emotion. Hearers might be aware of a very different system practiced by their loved ones. We can only be sensitive to their concern, and try to point them to the love and justice of God, as well as to how one is saved, by faith in the Gospel of Christ, found in 1 Corinthians 15:1-4.

OBJECTION 27

"I believe in me."
"I have my own beliefs."
"You have your way; I have mine."
"Let's agree to disagree."
"All religions are equal; let's co-exist."

It can be challenging to witness to those who seem to be okay with everything. They aren't offended by the Gospel of Christ. They aren't threatened by it, and they don't seem concerned. They may have "faith" in everything or in nothing. They deny faith in Christ, not out of hostility, but out of apathy. They just want everyone to get along. As Christians, we are not refusing to "co-exist" by testifying to the truth. We desire that others be saved so they can know the joy, love, peace, and hope that salvation provides.

> ... Behold the Lamb of God, which taketh away the sin of the world. (Jn 1:29b)

The "okay-with-everything" person may listen, therefore providing an opportunity for a witness to try to cultivate in him some concern for his future. This can be done by asking him if he thinks he has ever done anything wrong, and if he thinks that there may be accountability in the end for having done so. Someday we will all face death. If an afterlife exists, how does this objector plan to find its location and get there? If he believes in life after death, and in the meaningfulness of our life here, he might recognize that he has a few spots on his record, and that knowing how to access salvation is more important than he realized.

If this objector knows something of other philosophies and ideas of religion, he can be reminded that none have a solution to the problem of sin. If he does not know the differences among religions, a few basic facts about the major ones can be shared to demonstrate the impossibility of all their contradictory claims being true. It is not necessary to be an expert on world religion. Who God is, for example, can be presented as a simple comparison. The God of the Bible is a tri-unity; three persons exist in one spirit. Allah, the god of Islam, is a single god, alone in eternity. Buddhism has no personal god, while Hinduism claims that "all is god," expressed in millions of deities. Just that small amount of information makes the point that God cannot simultaneously be all these things. From there, the conversation can move to whether these "gods" provide evidence regarding the claims of their respective religious systems. If there is a creator and an afterlife, being right about how to gain salvation is of everlasting significance. Tolerance, acceptance, and belief in oneself are admirable principles, and they are useful for some things, but it is not wise to go your own way when you don't know where you are going.

OBJECTION 28

"I don't need to understand the Bible; I take it by faith."
"Faith is a blind leap, a leap in the dark."
"I hope I make it."

Some objections to faith as the way of salvation are not actually to faith, per se, but are due to a faulty definition of faith. Some objectors claim to have faith, but when asked about it, they describe it as a wish, not as a surety. A person with this view does not correctly understand faith, which must be directed at an object. In other words, faith is placed *in* something, such as a promise made by God. Faith in the Gospel of Christ is a conviction of mind regarding how one is saved, with the death, burial, and resurrection of Jesus Christ for sins as the object of faith.

The Bible defines faith as being "fully persuaded" that the facts being presented are true:

> *And being fully persuaded that, what He had promised, He was also able to perform.* (Ro 4:21)

> *These all died in faith, not having received the promises, but having seen them afar off, and were persuaded of them, and embraced them, and confessed that they were strangers and pilgrims on the earth.* (Heb 11:13)

> *Knowing therefore the terror of the Lord, we persuade men; but we are made manifest unto God; and I trust also are made manifest in your consciences.* (2 Cor 5:11)

The Bible also teaches us that faith has substance and evidence:

Now faith is the substance of things hoped for, the evidence of things not seen. (Heb 11:1)

Each of us is to believe the good news of salvation because it is reasonable and true:

And he reasoned in the synagogue every Sabbath, and persuaded the Jew and the Greeks. (Acts 18:4; see also Acts 19:8, 28:23)

And that we may be delivered from unreasonable and wicked men: for all men have not faith. (2 Thes 3:2)

Unfortunately, some 19th century German philosophy seeped into Christian theology, promoting the idea that faith is a "leap." This idea is a perversion of biblical faith and is, in fact, the opposite of faith. The Bible describes itself as "God-breathed," and its truthfulness is evident. Its salvation message is not, "Maybe you'll get to heaven, so cross your fingers." Salvation by grace through faith is presented as a surety, and each hearer must come to a conviction as to whether or not he will trust it.

… Abraham believed God, and it was accounted to him for righteousness. (Gal 3:6)

_____

_____

_____

OBJECTION 29

"I don't know."
"Nobody can know."

This objection to faith for salvation is either an admission that an individual does not know what is true, or a denial that anybody can know what is true. Those who describe themselves as agnostic typically mean that they personally do not know what is true about God or salvation. Others take this further, ironically refuting the absolute claims of the Bible by making another absolute claim: that truth cannot be known by anyone. "How do you personally know that nobody else can know?" is a powerful question to ask a person who holds the latter view. It can be reasoned that if we cannot know that something is true, then neither can we know it is not true. Therefore, it could be true. If the hearer will accept this logic, he may be willing to consider the declaration of Romans 1:19 that God has revealed Himself to man, and, therefore, His revelation about how to be saved can be known.

> *These things have I written unto you that believe on the name of the Son of God; that ye may know that ye have eternal life, and that ye may believe on the name of the Son of God.* (1 Jn 5:13)

OBJECTION 30

"I already believe in God; I don't need all those details."
"You're being picky. Just believe in Jesus."

Sometimes an objection to faith in the Gospel is characterized by an apparent aversion to defining terminology. Because salvation is by faith, one's faith must be placed in the correct object. Faith in the Gospel is not a general, nebulous belief, such as a belief in some "higher power" with no particular traits; therefore, one cannot believe the Gospel of Christ without knowing its elements.

> *For if he that cometh preacheth another Jesus, whom we have not preached, or if ye receive another spirit, which ye have not received, or another gospel, which ye have not accepted, ye might well bear with him.* (2 Cor 11:4)

Christians who stand up for an accurate Gospel are sometimes accused of being picky or "legalistic," as though a clear and thorough Gospel presentation is the equivalent of adding law-works for salvation, an issue covered in Chapter 4. While there are those who promote legalistic requirements for salvation, the Gospel itself is a message, and a message is either transmitted accurately or inaccurately. To deny this is to put oneself in the odd position of defending inaccuracy. We, as authors, believe it is not "picky" to handle God's word carefully and share the Gospel accurately. The many objections within this book show that the Gospel can be misunderstood in a startling number of ways. The hearer who objects that it is good enough to "just believe in Jesus" needs to be pointed back to the Bible as the authority, and its explanation of who Jesus is, what he did, and why. To emphasize the point, he can be asked, for example, "If you only need to believe in Jesus, then my question is, Jesus who?" The reason for asking this is because every counterfeit Christian group has a fake Jesus, such as the Mormon "Jesus" who is a brother to Lucifer, and the Jesus of Jehovah's Witnesses, who is a created being. Other examples of fakes include the Jesus of the Koran, who sneaked off the cross, and the Jesus of present-day Judaism, who was sneaked out of his grave. Saving faith is in the Jesus of the Bible, not a generic "Jesus" who cannot save. The Bible states that there is another Jesus and another gospel, which is a warning not to be taken lightly. Genuine faith in the Gospel of Christ is believing the particulars of its saving message. No Christian witness should be ashamed of providing a detailed and accurate explanation of the Gospel.

OBJECTION 31

"I was born a _____, and I'll die a _____."
"There are so many denominations; how do I know yours is right?"

Sometimes a person may object to faith in the Gospel of Christ because he believes that the one witnessing is trying to get him to change his denominational affiliation or to sever him from his beloved family church. But salvation is by faith—not by any particular church group—and any Christian denomination

> What saith the scripture?

or assembly can contain both believers and unbelievers. The Gospel should be shared with any person who does not seem to understand it, or who is willing to hear, regardless of where he attends church, or whether he does at all.

To remove denominational differences as the issue in a witnessing situation, the hearer can be shown that the testimony of the Bible is what matters, not the particulars of a denomination. But what if the denomination is a problem? Sometimes it is the elements of the Gospel itself which suggest to the hearer that his church or denomination has issues. If so, emphasize that the Bible is the authority, and suggest that his pastor is best suited to explain why his teachings contradict historic Christianity and the biblical record, if indeed they do.

This objection could turn into a debate about denominations themselves, but God does not recognize denominations; He recognizes His children, those who believe the Gospel of Christ (1 Cor 15:1-4). In 1 Corinthians 1:10-13, Paul admonishes the church for dividing and following individuals and emphasizes that the Gospel is what matters. Many denominations believe the same fundamentals of the faith. The differences between them might be many or few, but for the purpose of this book, the issue of denominations is whether their differences affect one's salvation.

There is neither Jew nor Greek, there is neither bond nor free, there is neither male nor female: for ye are all one in Christ Jesus. (Gal 3:28)

_____

_____

_____

OBJECTION 32

"I'm a Christian, but I don't believe in that 'born-again' stuff."

This objection to how one is saved could be a misunderstanding of terminology or a denial of what the term "born again" represents. Faith in the Gospel results in a spiritual birth, also known as being born again.

> *Jesus answered and said unto him, Verily, verily, I say unto thee, Except a man be born again, he cannot see the kingdom of God... Marvel not that I said unto thee, Ye must be born again.* (Jn 3:3, 7)

Many church attendees are unfamiliar with the idea of being born again and might simply be in need of an explanation. Reviewing the who, what, why, and how of the Gospel message might reveal that this person needs salvation. It could also show that he has already accepted the Gospel by faith, but has not been taught the terminology of his spiritual birth. More about the spiritual birth can be found in Chapter One of this book.

> *Blessed be the God and Father of our Lord Jesus Christ, who according to His great mercy has caused us to be born again to a living hope through the resurrection of Jesus Christ from the dead...* (1 Pet 1:3 NASB)

> *Being born again, not of corruptible seed, but of incorruptible, by the word of God, which liveth and abideth for ever.* (1 Pet 1:23)

OBJECTION 33

"You have to repent."
"You need to turn from sin."
"Faith alone is 'easy-believism.'"

Some objections to the teaching of faith alone for salvation amount to a difference in the use of words and their definitions, such as in the disagreements among some Christians regarding the word "repent." We, as writers, believe that the concept of repentance is embedded within the meaning of saving faith; it is a change of mind from what was previously believed to agreement with the Gospel message. Some think, however, that repentance is a change of behavior, describing it as "turning from sin." This definition implies a moral reform, which is contrary to gracious salvation.

The problem with adding to the Gospel a promise of future behavioral improvement is that grace excludes works, and, therefore, the Gospel of Christ cannot include a performance standard.

Additionally, no human being can promise what his future behavior will be. He may have good intentions, but that is no guarantee and, therefore, cannot

> Of his own will begat he us with the word of truth ... (Jas 1:18a)

be part of salvation, as it would make our status with God unknown and unknowable. Furthermore, the idea that one must "turn from sin" to be saved is impossible. If any person must enumerate his sins and then turn from them to get saved, he would never get saved nor would anyone. An unsaved person is spiritually dead; he cannot turn from sin nor obey the command to live according to God's will. Even if "turning from sin" is defined only as a mental determination to obey God, it still adds a requirement that is not in the Gospel of Christ. Although a general awareness of being separated from God because of sin is implied by the fact that we need a savior, God does not require us to make any promises of future behavior in order to be saved.

Salvation is not "cleaning up your act," "turning over a new leaf," or "determining to forsake sin." Salvation is a spiritual birth resulting from believing the contents of a message, the Gospel of Christ. Recognizing sin and allowing the Holy Spirit to empower a God-honoring Christian life is part of maturity after one is saved.

If this objection is not about the particulars of repentance, it may be about salvation being by grace and nothing else, covered in Chapter 4. Listening and learning what a person means by repentance allows a Christian witness to correctly address the "how" of salvation and explain biblical repentance. Convinced that there is something more to salvation than just believing a message, an objector may call salvation by faith alone "easy-believism." Some hearers cannot believe that the Gospel is so simple and pure. But it has to be pure; it cannot be tainted with the works of a sinner. The phrase "by which also ye are saved," found in Paul's Gospel presentation makes it plain that its elements are sufficient to save.

Whosoever believeth that Jesus is the Christ is born of God...
(1 Jn 5:1a)

_____

_____

_____

"If you think you can just believe on your own, that's decisional regeneration—you think you saved yourself with your decision."
"If I have to exercise faith, that's a work."
"We are too depraved by sin to believe."
"I was chosen."

If you hear this objection to faith for salvation, you could be speaking with a religiously sophisticated person who is unsaved, or from a Christian who follows a particular brand of theology. Your aim as a Christian witness is to ascertain whether this person's faith is in the idea of having been chosen, or if it is in the work of Jesus on the cross.

> So then faith cometh by hearing ... (Ro 10:17a)

Some believe that man is incapable of responding to the Gospel because being a sinner, he cannot exercise saving faith. Because the Bible calls us to hear and believe, our view as writers is that there is a difference between "deciding" and "believing." We do not agree that the call to believe is the equivalent of saving oneself through a decision. By defining faith as the Bible does, as being persuaded of facts, we are not deciding to believe, but have been convinced by God's word and the Holy Spirit that the Gospel of Christ is true.

> *For what saith the scripture? Abraham believed God, and it was counted unto him for righteousness....He staggered not at the promise of God through unbelief; but was strong in faith, giving glory to God; And being fully persuaded that, what he had promised, he was able also to perform. And therefore it was imputed to him for righteousness.* (Ro 4:3, 20-22)

Another variation of this objection is the contention that salvation's one condition—faith—amounts to "doing something" to get saved. This view considers faith itself to be a work. When we believe, however, we are not "doing" anything, because the Bible specifically excludes faith as a work. It, in fact, contrasts faith and work as opposites:

> *But to him that worketh not, but believeth on him that justifieth the ungodly, his faith is counted for righteousness.* (Ro 4:5)

Faith in the Gospel of Christ is not a work done by me, but the recognition that somebody else did something for me, namely that Jesus died on the cross to pay for my sins (1 Cor 15:1-4).

OBJECTION 35

"Yes, I'm saved … as long as …" (…I don't turn my back on Jesus … I don't sin too much … I don't commit the unpardonable sin … I don't fall away … I keep believing … I repent when I sin.)

A "what-if" type of objection to faith is an outcome-based belief for which faith is not the determining factor of salvation. Salvation is secure only "if" one avoids some sins, limits others, or quickly repents afterward. Rejecting faith alone for salvation is ultimately a form of legalism, covered in Chapter 4; in this view, one's status as a Christian is not dependent upon the satisfactory sacrifice of

Jesus, but upon oneself. Committing a particular sin cancels the payment He made on the cross.

Another version of this objection to the "how" of salvation is something we call "fruit inspection," meaning that salvation is determined by whether or not a person is bearing fruit. If he is not, he has lost his salvation or was never saved at all. The problem with this notion quickly becomes apparent when the objector is asked to define fruit, to quantify the amount and frequency of fruit needed to prove salvation, and by what calculation it will be measured.

> The Christian life is not a maintenance plan to stay saved.

These "what-if" objections make the Christian life into a maintenance plan to stay saved, as if the sacrifice of Christ was not sufficient to do so. One must keep bearing fruit or be careful to avoid certain sins in order to stay saved. There is no security in such a system; if our sins are not fully paid, we aren't actually saved from anything. According to this objection, Christians continue to be at risk of hell, making the entire concept of "being saved" meaningless.

The source of this objection is sometimes due to confusion between God's parental discipline of the believer and the final judgment of the unsaved. Bible verses which relate to the Christian's loss of rewards are misunderstood to mean a loss of one's saved status. The Bible, however, teaches that

> If Christians remain at risk of hell, "salvation" is meaningless.

believers are "sealed unto the day of redemption" by the Holy Spirit, Himself, and we are, therefore, secure. The question for this objector is, "If you did turn your back on Jesus, isn't that just another sin He paid for?"

Now he which stablisheth us with you in Christ, and hath anointed us, is God; Who hath also sealed us, and given the earnest of the Spirit in our hearts. (2 Cor 1:21-22)

In whom ye also trusted, after that ye heard the word of truth, the gospel of your salvation: in whom also after that ye believed, ye were sealed with that holy Spirit of promise... (Eph 1:13)

And grieve not the holy Spirit of God, whereby ye are sealed unto the day of redemption. (Eph 4:30)

The Bible verse which warned Israel to do "fruit inspection" had nothing to do with the Christian life. It was a call to recognize the false prophecies of false prophets:

Beware of false prophets, which come to you in sheep's clothing, but inwardly they are ravening wolves. Ye shall know them by their fruits. (Mt 7:15-16a; see also 2 Pet 2:1)

Believers are to walk in holiness, bear fruit, and repent if they fall into sin. Doing such things, however, does not determine salvation. They are a result of salvation, and a product of spirituality as a Christian learns and grows in the faith. How we are saved is by grace through faith. The grace that saves us also keeps us. If it did not, what Jesus provided on the cross cannot be considered salvation.

Now unto him that is able to keep you from falling, and to present you faultless before the presence of his glory with exceeding joy ... (Jude 1:24)

OBJECTION 36

"Yes, I'm saved; I _____." (… prayed the sinner's prayer … was baptized … was confirmed … went forward at an altar call … asked Jesus into my heart … gave my life to Jesus … made a decision for Christ … made Jesus the Lord of my life … promised to follow Jesus.)

Some responses to discussions of faith are not so much objections as they are a failure to distinguish between faith and a church activity or ceremony which accompanied faith. This is sometimes due to well-intentioned people who have developed creative ways to explain or provide "easier access" to the Gospel … other than just explaining the Gospel. An example of this is the ubiquitous "Ask Jesus into your heart." Making such a statement might or might not accompany an understanding of the Gospel. Doing so, however, is not the equivalent of believing the content of the Gospel of Christ, and in many cases has given false hope to someone who made the request but does not understand the who, what, why, and how of the Gospel.

Similarly, the use of popular Christian phrases, such as "following Jesus" or "giving your life to Jesus," are treated as if they are the equivalent of the Gospel of Christ. Short-cut phrases without definitions are not intended to obscure the Gospel, but they can and do.

When speaking with someone who gives a testimony which adds a condition to faith in the Gospel of Christ, ask him to explain his conversion experience and learn as much as possible about what he thinks saved him. Does he, for example, think that the prayer he prayed saved him? Does he think he would be saved had he not been baptized with water, publicly confessed Christ, or done some other added work? Rather than debating the efficacy of baptism or some other tradition, bring the discussion back to the content of the Gospel and its call to simply believe.

Going through the elements of the Gospel will often reveal if this objector's faith is misplaced, as well as help him to see that the activity or ritual in question is not included in its message. Sinners are not offering Almighty God anything; we are asked to accept what *He* did. In faith, we look away from our own perceived goodness and self-righteousness, and recognize the work of another. No

> When a person is asked to do something to be saved, his faith will be in what he did.

works done, no goodness maintained, no sin repented of, or prayer sincerely prayed can save us. Only Jesus saves, and He saves through the Gospel message, by faith, stated plainly in 1 Corinthians 15:1-4.

Forasmuch as ye know that ye were not redeemed with corruptible things, as silver and gold, from your vain conversation received by tradition from your fathers; But with the precious blood of Christ, as of a lamb without blemish and without spot: Who verily was foreordained before the foundation of the world, but was manifest in these last times for you, Who by him do believe in God, that raised him up from the dead, and gave him glory; that your faith and hope might be in God. (1 Pet 1:18-21)

_____

_____

_____

SIX

WHERE TO FIND IT

The Bible

A t least eighty verses in the Bible include the phrase, "it is written;" God continually directs us to His written word. An objection about the Bible is an objection to the Gospel's source of authority. Without the record of the Bible, we have no authoritative source of information about God. God chose the written word to create a record of His communication with mankind. In comparing this written record with his miraculous experiences, Peter calls the scripture "a more sure word of prophecy," preserving God's message throughout time (2 Pet 1:19). John warns that those who "believeth not the record that God gave of his Son" are calling God a liar (1 Jn 5:10b).

It is helpful for Christian witnesses to be aware of the many ways in which the unsaved can object to the elements of the Gospel. Our familiarity can make us better prepared to answer objections when we ask someone a question about their faith—or lack of it. For example, some objections to the Bible are merely bait for an argument or parroted criticisms; having no convictions of his own, the objector who denies the Bible's reliability might be willing to hear the Gospel if his objections are answered.

Trusting the Bible matters because it is where the message of salvation is found. If a hearer rejects the Bible as God's word, offering verses or asking him to place his faith in its message may be premature, and may even harden his resolve to oppose it. We do not recommend pressing a person who is not open. A willingness to consider the

> ... according to the scriptures ...

evidence of the Bible's trustworthiness, and a recognition of it as a reliable source of information is an important foundation for believing the Gospel of Christ, found in 1 Corinthians 15:1-4.

OBJECTION 37

"The Bible is full of errors and contradictions."
"It couldn't possibly be the same Bible after 2000 years."
"It has been changed by the translators."
"There is no way that _____ happened."

When an objector claims that the Bible has mistakes and translation problems, he should be asked to cite them. "Could you tell me to which verses you are referring?" If he is unable to offer any contradictory verses or erroneous information, he may drop his objection and be willing to hear. The bottom line, after all, is that the Creator of the universe is able to

> The Creator of the universe is able to preserve His book.

preserve His book. However, if he is a studied objector and is able to voice examples for which you have no explanation, do not feel that you must have an immediate answer. You can offer to do some research and get back to him. If he is interested in further study regarding the historical accuracy, supernatural origin, and meticulous preservation of the Bible, there are many books on the subject. If he is not willing to consider the authority of the Bible, he is unlikely to be open to its saving message. We offer the truth; God will work on his heart.

> *You performed signs and wonders in Egypt and have continued them to this day, in Israel and among all mankind, and have gained the renown that is still yours.* (Jer 32:20 NIV)

> *But the word of the Lord endureth for ever. And this is the word which by the gospel is preached unto you.* (1 Pet 1:25)

OBJECTION 38

"It's a good book, but it's not inspired."
"It was written by men."

Most Christians have probably heard the old canard that the Bible was written only by men. Some of the same people who believe that there is a "psychic connection" between thinking about a friend and then receiving a call from him, find it hard to believe that God could inspire a person to write a letter. This objector probably does not realize that he is putting himself in the role of Bible expert with his denial of its divine origin. Since the Bible says that it is inspired by God, this objection is one of those occasions when a hearer simply has to decide for himself if he believes the record of scripture, or if he is interested enough to learn more about the evidence of its supernatural character. A

> All scripture is given by inspiration of God … (2 Tim 3:16a)

Christian witness can ask the hearer if he would like to see what the Bible says about itself, offering verses which show that the doctrine of the inspiration of scripture is not a matter of opinion, but a foundation of Christianity:

> *For the prophecy came not in old time by the will of man: but holy men of God spake as they were moved by the Holy Ghost.* (2 Pet 1:21)

OBJECTION 39

"That's your opinion; this is what it means to me."
"You can make the Bible mean anything you want."

Some of those who are presented with the Gospel hold the opinion that the Bible is a nice inspirational book, but its contents are only a matter of opinion. Those who have had some exposure to the Bible might have a favorite verse or passage which has been assigned a personal interpretation, but has no other significance.

The underlying objection to the Gospel could be one of many, and will hopefully be uncovered with further discussion.

In addressing the objection to Bible meaning, the point needs to be made that every word has a definition, and cannot mean "anything you want." If it were not so, people would not be able to communicate with each other at all. For example, if he opened a cookbook and looked at a recipe, could he make it mean anything? The answer is obvious.

You could receive a follow-up objection which is that many words have multiple meanings. This is true, but even so, a word's meaning is narrowed by both its immediate and, in the case of the Bible, its historical context. If asked, the objector who makes this claim will not be able to produce a Bible passage that can "mean anything." Using the Gospel passage as an example, you can show him that there is little room for variation in its interpretation.

In some cases, this objection is related to the differences among various Christian denominations. As Christian witnesses ourselves, we have encountered hearers who are distressed by the existence of so many kinds of churches and the differences between them. We know, of course, that the fact that Christians disagree on the finer points of the faith is a far cry from being able to make the Bible mean anything. We can provide assurance that although we all have much to learn, the death, burial, and resurrection of Jesus Christ for sins is what saves us, and on that point, Christians agree.

> Every word has a definition, and cannot mean "anything you want."

Knowing this first, that no prophecy of the scripture is of any private interpretation. (2 Pet 1:20)

OBJECTION 40

"I Just Don't Believe It."

Some with whom you speak will just say, "No." A person who will not assent to even the historical facts of the Gospel is probably not open to placing his faith in it. Others are not interested or do not care enough to even formulate an objection. This could be because they have not thought about it, or because they are not ready to get into the discussion. Offer what you can. If someone is not willing to hear, respect his feelings about it, perhaps asking him to talk again sometime in the future. Pursuing a discussion with someone who does not want to hear is not helpful for your relationship with him, for your testimony, or for the likelihood that he will be open in the future. It can be disappointing, aggravating and even painful to be shut down when you want to share good news, but God protects his freedom to disbelieve, even allowing him to be blinded from something that is so clearly true.

> *In whom the god of this world hath blinded the minds of them which believe not, lest the light of the glorious gospel of Christ, who is the image of God, should shine unto them.* (2 Cor 4:4)

Remember that the Lord, in His boundless longsuffering and mercy, wants this person to be saved even more than you do. If he becomes willing to trust the source of the Gospel and hear it, we can rest in the assurance that our God is good; those who desire to know the truth will eventually be saved (2 Co 3:15-16).

Who will have all men to be saved, and to come unto the knowledge of the truth. (1 Tim 2:4)

_____

_____

_____

CONCLUSION

IT IS GOD WHO SAVES

… The LORD God, merciful and gracious, longsuffering,
and abundant in goodness and truth … (Ex 34:6b)

B
elieving that we had heard it all, we, the authors, challenged a friend to give us an objection that was not in this book. She did. In fact, she had just heard it. An ailing, elderly person to whom she had been witnessing told her that he did not want to accept the Gospel because he was afraid that if he did, he would die right then. She was confounded by his response, and we both admitted we had not heard it before. Upon consideration, we concluded that a person afraid of dying has doubts as to whether the afterlife is better than this life. At its core, his fear is a doubt about the character of God and whether He is true to His promises—a "who He is" objection.

God is good, has a good intention for all of us, and will wait long for our repentance. God loved us in Christ, by sending the Son to die for all the sins of the world. Hopefully this hearer will be open to learning more about God's goodness. The eternal consequence of forfeiting the gift of salvation is so horrible that the idea of allowing someone to slip away without hearing it drives our efforts to be witnesses.

A passion for sharing the Gospel is a wonderful thing to have, and it is best tempered with the knowledge that we are often only seed-planters, and always servants. It is God who saves. We do what we can, but if someone isn't ready, or says, "No," there is no value in pressing him or in being hard on oneself about it. For some, the Gospel is a lot to take in; eternity is a lot to think about. New information often forms questions in a hearer's mind as he thinks of things he had no occasion to consider before. We have spoken with people who genuinely do not know what they believe. After hearing the Gospel, or even simply being asked a question about it, they needed time to think and process our conversation before they had any response to it at all.

We can trust our good God to make every effort to save. Sometimes the process is a long one, and we as Christian witnesses might never see the result. But we can rest in the knowledge that the Holy Spirit is doing His part, convincing the hearer of the truths presented. God wants our spouse, child, loved

> And let us not be weary in well doing: for in due season we shall reap, if we faint not. (Gal 6:9)

one, and friend to be saved much more than we do! If they are open to the Gospel, they will come to believe it.

The Gospel by which we are saved is clearly articulated in 1 Corinthians 15:3-4, within the context of verses 1-8. When we share it but do not receive the desired response, offering a "short-cut" to the hearer can be tempting, but we must never stray from God's saving message. Encouraging a "decision for Christ" or leading a prayer might seem harmless, but such things can be made *without understanding*. Eliciting an on-the-spot profession can short-circuit the process of allowing the hearer to thoughtfully consider the reasonableness of the Gospel. It can also interfere with the ministry of the Holy Spirit to convict the hearer of sin and convince him of the truth.

The Gospel of Christ is not a formula, or an incantation, or "magic words" that one can say to be saved. Neither is God's word a secondary source to confirm a sign or an experience. A person who imagines that he has become a believer because he has witnessed a miracle, for example, has only

> A prayer can be made for salvation without understanding the Gospel.

become a believer in the miracle. The Gospel of Christ, found in 1 Corinthians 15:1-4, is a particular message which one must believe in order to receive the gift of salvation.

Every word of scripture is God-breathed. We must handle, speak, and share God's word with accuracy, as the holy gift from heaven that it is. We may need to educate our Christian friends about the importance of doing so. We may face persecution as we attempt to engage both Christians and non-Christians into conversations about the Gospel and other Bible topics, but we can stand against the "politically correct" social rules which intimidate Christians into silence. We can and should talk about important matters, whether of this world, or of the next. We need not bow to the Ruler of this Age whose singular purpose is to thwart the blessings of God to mankind. He will not ultimately succeed, but neither will we give him aid. Sometimes our efforts will succeed, sometimes not. We share the Gospel. It is God who saves.

"Ruthie"

At least annually for twenty years, a friend of ours heard the Gospel from one of us or from both. She was known for charitable giving within her community. She helped her neighbors and helped at church. She made contributions to college scholarships and made quilts for the homeless. She

> ... One soweth, and another reapeth. (John 4:37b)

certainly would not have made a silly claim such as that her quilt-making, for example, was a ticket into heaven, and yet she believed in a general sense that doing good works is part of a person's qualification to get there. Ruthie was a religious unbeliever.

When we visited, we never had to ask her a question to get into a conversation about the Gospel. During every visit, Ruthie asked us questions about the Bible and wanted to talk about salvation. Every time we explained the saving message, she had the same response: "I can't believe I don't have to do anything." It bothered her and she had no peace, so we had essentially the same conversation year after year:

"What about the verses on works? I can't believe I don't have to do anything."

"But that is what grace is. It literally means "undeserved favor" and God is exercising grace by saving us. If we had to do works to get salvation, it would not be a gift. It would not be undeserved; it would be earned. When you earn something, the one you work for is indebted to you. They owe you for the work you did. Do you think that you can indebt God to you? Do you think you can stand before Him on judgment day and tell Him that you were good and so He owes you heaven?"

"Well, no, that seems presumptuous. But so does assuming that I can just get in for nothing."

"You aren't getting in for nothing. You were given a gift by someone who did the work for you. You are accepting what Jesus did on your behalf. He did the work, so to speak, and it wasn't nothing."

"But I believe that."

"Yes, but you don't believe that what He did is enough. You think that you have to do something."

"So, what about all the things in the Bible that God says He wants us to do?"

"Well, He does want us to do good things. But those things are not a way to get into heaven. Good works are a result of salvation. The way into heaven is by believing the Gospel of Christ. Faith in what Jesus did on the cross for sin is the method God provided for our salvation."

"What about the people who do really bad things?"

"We all rebel against God, and God considers all rebellion 'really bad.' But those sins were all paid on the cross. There are not some sins that are excluded from 'the sins of the world.' It includes everything. If it is available to the whole world, then it can't be about how good or bad someone is. If it is about believing in Him, then it can't be about what you or I do. Even if I do lots of wonderful things, it doesn't erase or wipe out my sins. Once I've sinned against God, I can't make up for it. I can't travel back in time and undo it or fix it. So, I already deserve the penalty for sin, no matter how many good things I do. Jesus Christ didn't have any sins on His account, so He was a pure and perfect sacrifice for sin. He paid for those sins for us, and all He asks is that we trust in His payment. That is faith; it is being persuaded that the Gospel is true, that Jesus died on the cross for your sins, and was buried and rose again, just as the Bible foretold."

"So, I don't have to do anything?"

"No."

"Just believe it?"

"Yes."

"Even Hitler could get in?"

"Yes."

"I can't believe I don't have to do anything."

"I know."

A few weeks before she passed away, at 95 years old, she made a rare telephone call to us. She said, "I haven't been able to stop thinking about you. Will you be coming to visit?" She knew her life was nearly over and eternity was on her mind. Having just seen her three weeks earlier, we quickly made arrangements for another seven-hundred-mile drive to her home, hoping for one last chance to testify. Always having been fascinated with prophecy, she was a longtime viewer of the Jack Van Impe television show. She admired him because he knew so much scripture by heart. When we arrived, she was eager to tell us that she had written to Van Impe with her question, the same question she asked us every time we visited. She was very proud to say that he had written back. When he confirmed what she had heard so many times, that she was saved by faith alone, she finally believed, telling us, "Now I know that Jesus did it all."

So shall my word be that goeth forth out of my mouth: it shall not return unto me void, but it shall accomplish that which I please, and it shall prosper in the thing whereto I sent it. (Isa 55:11)

The Lord is not slack concerning his promise, as some men count slackness; but is longsuffering to us-ward, not willing that any should perish, but that all should come to repentance. (2 Pet 3:9)

APPENDIX

INDEX OF OBJECTIONS

ABOUT THE AUTHORS

Preston Condra, M.Div., graduated from Oklahoma Baptist University and Southwestern Baptist Theological Seminary. He has been preaching, teaching, lecturing, writing, and appearing on broadcasts for more than twenty-five years. His wife Kelly, M.S.Ed., has been teaching and speaking throughout her career. Together, they founded Sufficient Word Ministries and have authored many books.

sufficient WORD
MINISTRIES

www.sufficientword.com